Computing Professionals
Changing Needs for the 1990s

A Workshop Report Prepared by the
Steering Committee on Human Resources
in Computer Science and Technology

Computer Science and Telecommunications Board
Commission on Physical Sciences,
Mathematics, and Applications

and

Office of Scientific and Engineering Personnel

National Research Council

D1456783

NATIONAL ACADEMY PRESS
Washington, D.C.   1993

NOTICE: The project that is the subject of this report was approved by the Governing Board of the National Research Council, whose members are drawn from the councils of the National Academy of Sciences, the National Academy of Engineering, and the Institute of Medicine. The members of the steering committee responsible for the report were chosen for their special competences and with regard for appropriate balance.

This report has been reviewed by a group other than the authors according to procedures approved by a Report Review Committee consisting of members of the National Academy of Sciences, the National Academy of Engineering, and the Institute of Medicine.

Support for this project was provided by the Defense Advanced Research Projects Agency (Grant No. N00014-87-J-1110), the National Science Foundation (Grant No. CDA-9121558), and the Association for Computing Machinery, the Computer and Business Equipment Manufacturers Association, the Information Technology Association of America, and the Institute of Electrical and Electronics Engineers (under unnumbered contracts).

Available from:
National Academy Press
2101 Constitution Avenue, N.W.
Washington, D.C. 20418

B-030

Printed in the United States of America

The National Academy of Sciences is a private, nonprofit, self-perpetuating society of distinguished scholars engaged in scientific and engineering research, dedicated to the furtherance of science and technology and to their use for the general welfare. Upon the authority of the charter granted to it by Congress in 1863, the Academy has a mandate that requires it to advise the federal government on scientific and technical matters. Dr. Frank Press is president of the National Academy of Sciences.

The National Academy of Engineering was established in 1964, under the charter of the National Academy of Sciences, as a parallel organization of outstanding engineers. It is autonomous in its administration and in the selection of its members, sharing with the National Academy of Sciences the responsibility for advising the federal government. The National Academy of Engineering also sponsors engineering programs aimed at meeting national needs, encourages education and research, and recognizes the superior achievements of engineers. Dr. Robert M. White is president of the National Academy of Engineering.

The Institute of Medicine was established in 1970 by the National Academy of Sciences to secure the services of eminent members of appropriate professions in the examination of policy matters pertaining to the health of the public. The Institute acts under the responsibility given to the National Academy of Sciences by its congressional charter to be an adviser to the federal government and, upon its own initiative, to identify issues of medical care, research, and education. Dr. Kenneth I. Shine is president of the Institute of Medicine.

The National Research Council was organized by the National Academy of Sciences in 1916 to associate the broad community of science and technology with the Academy's purposes of furthering knowledge and advising the federal government. Functioning in accordance with general policies determined by the Academy, the Council has become the principal operating agency of both the National Academy of Sciences and the National Academy of Engineering in providing services to the government, the public, and the scientific and engineering communities. The Council is administered jointly by both Academies and the Institute of Medicine. Dr. Frank Press and Dr. Robert M. White are chairman and vice chairman, respectively, of the National Research Council.

Preface

At the invitation of the Office of Scientific and Engineering Personnel (OSEP), the Computer Science and Telecommunications Board (CSTB) joined OSEP in an exploratory project aimed at better understanding the human resource base of the computing profession. CSTB and OSEP convened a steering committee that combined computer scientists with social scientists who specialize in analyzing scientific and technical labor markets. The steering committee was charged with organizing a cross-disciplinary workshop, which was held on October 28-29, 1991, in Irvine, California, and developing this summary report of that workshop and the steering committee's subsequent deliberations, which were carried out primarily through numerous telephone, teleconference, and electronic mail interactions over the year following the workshop.

The workshop illustrated the value of bringing together people from a range of backgrounds—economics and other social sciences, computer science, and computer and electrical engineering; research, product development, management, and data analysis; and government, industry, and academia. The interaction of workshop participants reflected a range of perspectives, as well as areas of agreement and lack of agreement. It is in illuminating that range that this report makes its greatest contribution; it underscores the problems discussed at the workshop that arise from a lack of consensus both within and between segments of the computing professional community on issues as basic as what to call these professionals. The report attempts to define and focus attention on specific problems and approaches to solving them, identifying a range of steps that could be taken by federal statistical agencies, professional organizations, and others.

Appended to the report are three papers that were prepared and delivered as presentations at the workshop. They include information collected and evaluated by their respective authors. These papers were used as resources during the workshop and subsequently by the steering committee.

CSTB and OSEP are grateful for the financial support of the Association for Computing Machinery, the Computer and Business Equipment Manufacturers Association, the Information Technology Association of America, the Institute of Electrical and Electronics Engineers, the National Science Foundation, and the Defense Advanced Research Projects Agency, which made this project possible.

Contents

ix

Computing Professionals

Changing Needs for the 1990s

Executive Summary

Ensuring economic competitiveness and satisfying societal needs will depend increasingly on what people do with computer-based technology. Changes in that technology are having profound effects: the shift from large, centralized computing systems to smaller and distributed systems is fueling the growth in demand for computing systems and enabling the spread of computer-based technology into our everyday lives.

Skilled professionals, in turn, are responsible for developing and implementing computer-based technology and for its diffusion throughout our society. These highly skilled professionals are often treated as part of a large occupational group, a group that can be referred to as "computing professionals." But that label masks an unusually wide range of occupations, including researchers in computer science and computer engineering, developers of commercial applications and systems, and individuals involved in deploying applications and systems. And within these occupations are people with an unusually broad range of backgrounds. Adding to the confusion over the identity and number of computing professionals is the growing use of computing in other professional domains. However, professional users of computing systems should not be confused with computing professionals, who create, develop, or support computing technology and applications.

Maintaining U.S. excellence in the creation and use of computing systems requires access to a sufficient supply of the best talent. Because employers, educators, and public policymakers know so little about the size of the labor pool and the skill requirements and responsibilities of the individuals shaping the computer revolution, human resources planning and policymaking are more haphazard than they should be. Opportunities for achieving a better fit between supply and demand are being lost, and in an increasingly competitive global economy the consequences may be far-reaching.

WORKSHOP ORGANIZATION AND FINDINGS

Over the course of two days, the problems associated with trying to understand the scope and scale of computing professional occupations were discussed at a workshop convened by the Computer Science and Telecommunications Board and the Office of Scientific and Engineering Personnel of the National Research Council. The workshop was exploratory: its purpose was to assess what is and is not known about supply and demand for computing professionals; how perceptions about this labor market differ in industry, academia, and government; and what kinds of steps could be taken to advance knowledge and understanding of relevant issues. The workshop agenda and list of participants were developed by a steering committee, which framed the issues that participants were asked to discuss and deliberated over the comments and insights that were generated during the workshop. Participants in the workshop included academic computer scientists and engineers, managers of businesses developing and applying computing systems, and experts in human resources and labor economics. Participants were selected for their insights into real-world practice in these different arenas.

The steering committee found reasonable consensus among workshop participants about the following:

Demand Is Fluid and Skill Requirements Are Growing

• Demand for computing professionals is subject to strong crosscurrents that are masked by statistical averaging. Industries that have been major employers of computing professionals have been contracting; at the same time, the shift to smaller systems is stimulating growth in sales throughout most of the computer sector. To draw meaningful conclusions, trends in individual industries, occupations, and computing and communications technologies must be evaluated together.

• Based on their discussion of these trends, the steering committee and workshop participants concluded that demand for computing professionals is expected to grow overall, although more slowly than in the 1980s.

• The overall level of skill required in computing professional occupations appears to be growing. Increases in required skills are expected to affect most if not all of these professions. As skill requirements grow, employers may increase their demand for individuals with formal education in computer science and engineering.

• Demand for individuals in specific jobs and occupations appears to shift relatively frequently. So do the responsibilities and skill sets that define specific jobs, occupations, and the mix of occupations that characterize computing professional work. For example, while the popular image of a computing professional may be that of a "programmer," leaders in the development and application of computing systems now reserve that title for relatively less skilled jobs. Yet newer titles for software developers, such as "software engineer," are not necessarily used with any great precision.

• Demand for computing professionals to engage in research appears to be softening, observed workshop participants, due to constraints on funding for academic research and the decline of large central industrial research laboratories. Although individuals with training for or experience in research can be productively employed elsewhere, absent other changes the research component of the labor market may shrink.

Equality of Opportunity and the Increasingly Global Talent Pool Are Among Supply Challenges

• In general, given the current economic environment, the total supply of computing professionals is adequate for today's needs. Workshop participants acknowledged the existence of spot shortages in specific areas requiring specialized applications knowledge; also, almost by definition, skills involved in developing the leading edge of technology or its applications tend to be in tight supply. Participants from industry reported the greatest difficulty in meeting needs for software engineers.

• Given that bachelor's degree production is declining in science and engineering, especially in computer science, continuing attention will be needed to assure an adequate flow of talent into computing professional occupations. At issue are both the quantity and the quality of entrants.

- In particular, more effort should be made to encourage and support the interest of women and non-Asian minorities, groups that are underrepresented in the field. Underrepresented populations offer new sources of talent and new perspectives that can enrich the computing professions. Moreover, because these groups constitute growing proportions of the population, attracting them to computing professional occupations is essential for the survival of the field.
- The labor market for computing professionals is becoming increasingly global in scope. A large number of U.S. firms have begun to use computing professionals in other countries for a variety of research and development projects. And an increasing share of doctorates granted in this country are being awarded to foreign students, many of whom remain here.

Dynamic Occupations Require Continuous Learning

- Continuing education and training are important for computing professionals because of the dynamism of computing technologies and markets. Workshop participants observed that computing professionals need to become more aware of the importance of continuous learning. Support for continuing education is needed from educational institutions and employers, while individual employees may need encouragement to secure retraining periodically. The education of new entrants to computing professional occupations must provide a foundation for future training and retraining.

Better Planning Requires More and Better Data

- Better data are needed on the supply and demand for computing professionals. The dynamism of computing professional occupations makes it difficult to ensure that federal statistics about them remain accurate and sufficiently precise. Further problems arise from overlapping definitions of occupations and the tendency for different data sources to count different groups. A first step is to improve the taxonomies under which data are collected and analyzed, an effort that requires greater understanding of skill requirements and trends. Without a good categorization that reflects the actual division of labor in the work place and the actual differentiation among jobs by training or responsibility, there is a risk that too many distinct groups may be homogenized into overly broad categories. At the same time, there is a need for a robust high-level taxonomy with both a few broad occupational groupings and a clear explanation of associated portfolios of skills.

• Better data on education and degree production for computing professionals are needed to guide employers, students, educators, and policymakers. The large number and different types of apparently relevant education and training programs offered (computer science, computer engineering, information systems, information science, management of information systems, and so on) make it difficult to count the number of appropriately educated people and to target appropriate programs for study or hiring purposes.

THE CHALLENGE OF COMBINING VIEWPOINTS

While the workshop underscored the richness and excitement of computing professions, it also demonstrated the frustrations of attempting to discuss in common the rather different functions and concerns of researchers, applications and systems developers, and applications and systems deployers. Participants from academia and industry differed significantly in their perspectives, requirements, and concerns. Academic computer scientists and computer engineers, for example, argued for a narrower, more focused analysis of computer scientists and computer engineers. By contrast, a broader view was taken by managers of computing applications and systems development and deployment in industry and government. These workshop participants noted that they can meet most of their human resource needs, even for research, by hiring people without advanced education in computing (although these employees may need some form of advanced education and training). The discussions validated the notion that there is limited value in aggregating these professionals when analyzing the labor market.

Workshop participants emphasized the importance of continued interaction on issues relating to the supply and demand of computing professionals among employers, educators, and policymakers, in the interests of promoting a better fit between the supply and demand for computing professionals over the coming decade and beyond. Collaboration among all of these parties is essential for successful pursuit of a wide variety of next steps, such as those suggested in the concluding chapter of this report.

1

Introduction

Computing professionals constitute a broad and diverse group—theoreticians, people who design chips and hardware systems, developers of expert systems and databases, builders of information systems for banks and insurance companies, developers of software for personal computers, developers of hardware and software for local- and wide-area networks, and so on. In gross terms, this universe includes both designers and builders of hardware (engineers) and people concerned with making the hardware perform (scientists, engineers, and people who are not quite either). Not included are the growing numbers of people who use computing and communications systems in the course of pursuing other professions.

To better understand trends in the supply of and demand for computing professionals, the Computer Science and Telecommunications Board (CSTB) and the Office of Scientific and Engineering Personnel (OSEP) of the National Research Council convened an exploratory workshop. Understandably, given the complexity of the issues, the limited time available to workshop participants to address them, and the restricted attendance at the workshop, not all viewpoints were addressed; those addressed were not examined in equal depth; and it was not possible for participants to reach strong conclusions and to formulate detailed recommendations. Moreover, the views, requirements, and concerns of participants from academic computer science and engineering clearly differed from those of participants based in industry and government. Nonetheless, a number of notable findings emerged. This report summarizes the discussions at that workshop and the further deliberations of the steering committee that organized it.

The jobs, skills, and numbers of people associated with computing professionals are poorly understood. The reasons are many. First, the individuals who work in occupations associated with computing and who are variously aggregated as "computing professionals" are probably too heterogeneous to be meaningfully considered as belonging to one group. Asked Leslie L. Vadasz, senior vice president at Intel Corporation and chair of the workshop steering committee,

> Who is a computer specialist? Is it the scientist doing research in compiler technology or the engineer who is developing a game for a personal computer, or is it the MIS [management information systems] staff that manages our corporate information resources? They all are part of the profession, and there are many, many more who are also really part of this profession.

It is difficult to make useful generalizations, let alone forecasts, about such a diverse group. Nevertheless, attempts to do so are made regularly by people in government and industry; consequently, this report takes the aggregate of computing professionals as a point of departure.

Second, computing and communications systems technologies, applications, and markets are evolving quickly, resulting in a more rapid evolution in skill requirements, job design, and career paths than is the case for most other technical fields, such as physics, chemistry, and mathematics. One crude indicator of computing's rapid growth is the relative impermanence of job titles. For example, advances in software development have led to the emergence of jobs for highly skilled "software engineers"—people who design, develop, and maintain or modify complex software systems—and, simultaneously, to reduced opportunities for less-skilled programmers; now, some production of software code is even automated (that is, generated largely by computer systems).

Rapid changes in skill requirements are being compounded by changes in industrial employers, especially producers of computing and communications systems, who are a significant source of employment for computing professionals. These firms and industries have grown dramatically over the past 2 decades, and they have become increasingly international. At the same time, they have shifted from a primary emphasis on hardware to new emphases on software, networks, and systems. New technologies are fueling an overhaul of the computing infrastructure, which involves both a proliferation of hardware and significant amounts of software to make the hardware work. In addition, the computing environment is becoming much more distributed: computing is no longer concentrated among specialists or industries with large requirements for making calculations, and huge numbers of new users with varying levels of proficiency are driving the demand for and shape of information technology. These developments affect what is done by whom, where, and when.

Third, practitioners in the field have different perspectives on the various issues relating to computing professionals. For example, among computer science researchers in academia, computer systems developers and managers in industry and government (information resources managers), and personnel managers in organizations that produce and use computer technology, there is not even consensus on what to call different types of computing professionals or the group as a whole.

It is clear that computing professionals are an important group to understand because of their critical roles in improving and applying computer-based technologies. Thus, for example, one of the four components of the federal High Performance Computing and Communications program, the major national initiative in the computing field, is basic research and human resources. Explained Vadasz,

> [F]or us to make computer technology really ubiquitous, we must supply the profession with enough of the right talent to sustain growth. And to be able to do that, we must have a better understanding of who are the computer specialists. What do they do? How will their work change in the future? How do they get trained? How do they get educated? How do they get retrained? How could we make the supply better match the demand?

A fourth reason that computing professionals' skills and jobs are poorly understood is the lack of literature on the topic. These labor markets have not been rigorously studied in the way that other scientific and technical markets have. What information is available appears to consist of anecdotal evidence and data from surveys that have produced rather inconsistent results. Because of the absence of useful literature, workshop participants were selected to emphasize a broad set of practical experiences with the education, hiring, management, and training of computing professionals.

Combining comments made in workshop discussions with observations by the steering committee, this report presents the perspectives of workshop participants on issues in four major areas. Chapter 2 considers data (on employment and degree production) and taxonomy (categorization of jobs for use in collecting data), and it also discusses key concepts for measuring occupations. Chapter 3 considers overall demand for computing professionals and specific factors affecting demand in research, applications and systems development, and applications and systems deployment. Chapter 4 considers the supply of entrants to the field, describing educational programs and discussing demographic trends and needs. Chapter 5 considers implications for training and retraining of computing professionals in the labor market. The report concludes with a discussion in Chapter 6 of themes and next steps derived by the steering committee from the workshop discussions. Supporting material in the form of three presentations to the workshop is provided in Appendixes A, B, and C. Appendix D gives the program for the workshop. A survey of issues, the report identifies key questions, samples a range of opinions, and attempts to explain why it is that there are currently too few answers.

2

Data and Taxonomy: Computing Professionals Are Hard to Count

A number of methodological and taxonomic problems exist in attempting to produce data that accurately describe the supply, demand, and characteristics of computing professionals. This chapter summarizes the views and impressions of workshop participants about the strengths and limitations of available data for assessing the human resource base of the computer science and technology enterprise, focusing on inadequacies in the taxonomies used. It surveys the major available data sets, describes what the data show, and concludes with a discussion of the issues involved in improving on what is currently available.

INTRODUCTION

Accurate and timely information on the availability and utilization of computing professionals and their skills is vital to a wide variety of decisionmakers. Students choosing careers want to know about career opportunities and the nature of the work done by computing professionals. Policymakers need information to formulate proper programs of research, student support, and economic development. Academic employers want to know how easy it is to find people capable of teaching and doing fundamental research. Industrial and government employers are interested in knowing how easily they might recruit employees who can design, develop, or support computer systems.

Requirements for such information may be met in a variety of ways, for example, through the use of statistics generated in the many data collection efforts undertaken by governmental and nongovernmental organizations. While necessary, however, statistical information is not always sufficient. Many decisions involving human resources must be based on qualitative factors (e.g., personality, work experience, functional competencies) that are difficult to summarize in a data set. Moreover, no single set of information is able to satisfy the needs of all potential users. Recruiters for an individual company may need more detailed information than do those who formulate national policy on R&D or student support. Given the variety of data collection efforts and user needs, it is not surprising to find that the computing professions are one group for which, depending on one's perspective, there are no data, poor data, and/or conflicting data. Even in a very narrow category such as Ph.D.s in computer science, counts of the number of people differ.

WHY ARE THE DATA UNSATISFYING?

Current data on computing professionals reflect two classes of problems: (1) common difficulties encountered in gathering data and (2) uncommon disagreement about how to label and categorize computing professionals. Difficulties of the first type are largely methodological and include inconsistencies arising from differences in responding units (e.g., university registrars, personnel managers, individuals) as well as in how individuals might report when faced with alternative lists of fields, occupations, responsibilities, or skills.[1] Third-party counts typically do not agree with self-reporting counts, and discrepancies are compounded by the fact that data-gathering activities differ in focus and purpose, geographic scope, how nonrespondents are handled, sampling, and aggregation of data.

Data-gathering errors, although inevitable, are a special concern in analyzing occupations employing small numbers of people. In total, computing professional occupations, plus related technical occupations, appear to employ about 1 million workers, or less than 1 percent of the total U.S. work force—but also 7 percent of what the Bureau of Labor Statistics calls "professional specialty" occupations, a remarkable level for an occupational group that is less than 30 years old. Moreover, these occupations are changing dramatically, and this dynamism creates problems for classification and reporting. Commented Barbara Wamsley, deputy director, Federal Programs, National Academy of Public Administration, "By the time you get the standard written for the job, the job has changed."

Need for Agreement on Labeling

However, the biggest problem plaguing data collection efforts relates to labeling: i.e., what is a computer scientist, computer engineer, or other computing professional? This question has not been answered with consensus within the computing professional community, nor translated into common practice among data gatherers. The essential problem is to define what different kinds of computing professionals do. There is little agreement even within segments of the community as to the tasks, the skills and training required, or other defining parameters of the various computing occupations.

Absent a general consensus about what computing professionals do, it is difficult to attain agreement within the community on taxonomic labels. For example, academic researchers appear most likely to identify themselves as "computer scientists," but people in industry who have computer science degrees and are associated with systems design and development may have such job titles as "software engineer" or "systems integrator" and may report on themselves to data collectors according to these job titles. Members of the community cannot agree even on using the term *computer* in labeling computing professional occupations. Workshop participants involved in systems implementation in industry or government, for example, prefer "information systems" and "management" as elements of the overall label. As a result, there are serious differences among respondents, data sets, and analyses concerning what people would call individuals doing the same work, and a corresponding, almost overwhelming risk of comparing apples to oranges.

The newness of the computing field, the dramatic changes that it has been experiencing, and community members' lack of consensus on appropriate labeling thus come together to complicate the survey process. Explained Eileen Collins, senior sciences resources analyst at the National Science Foundation,

> When you are dealing with an evolutionary field, a number of problems turn up . . . . It is . . . hard to come up with an instrument that the people you are surveying will recognize as making the distinctions you want them to make. As a field develops and becomes more distinctly defined, it becomes easier. This is a field clearly undergoing continuing change. . . .
>
> [D]escriptions of the actual tasks in the job are important, so that respondents can, with a reasonably high degree of confidence, feel that they understand your question and that the answer they give is interpreted by them in the same way that you interpret it.

The greatest agreement on labeling seems to apply at both ends of the skill spectrum (taken most broadly). At the high end, "computer scientists" are typically associated with advanced education and the conduct of research. At the other end are workers who may be grouped with higher-level computing professionals in some counts but, because of the tasks involved or skills required, appear better classified as clerical (e.g., data entry) personnel—who are users of computer systems—or administrative support personnel (e.g., computer operators).[2]

Box 2.1 lists the computer-related occupations for which the Bureau of Labor Statistics (BLS) and the National Science Foundation (NSF) report data. Note that in contrast to such broad categories as "physical scientists" and "mathematicians," the listing includes titles representing a wide array of skills—computer systems analysts, computer programmers, computer operators and data entry personnel, hardware and software engineers, and various types of computer scientists. However, it is possible to identify the narrower set of occupations that approximately encompass the computing professionals focused on by workshop participants. The wide array of skills displayed in computer-related occupations is not unlike the broad range of skills characterizing health care practitioners—ranging from doctors and nurses to medical technicians. The similarity in breadth between these two taxonomies may reflect the dependence on a range of practitioners of these sectors of the U.S. work force.

Box 2.2 illustrates the commercial perspective on computing professional occupations, drawing from organizations that are major users of information technology. However, a different set of job titles might be composed for organizations focused on developing computer products (a list that might include developers of personal computer (PC) utilities, of distributed applications, and of local area network (LAN) and server software, as well as user interface designers, and so on). Further, noted Joe Kubat, vice president, Floor Systems, New York Stock Exchange, one would expect some differences in the set of job titles found in academic and other research environments as opposed to those found in business and other production organizations.

Community consensus on labeling is necessary not only to enable good data gathering and analysis at aggregate, national levels, but also to meet recruiting and training needs at the level of the firm or the institution of higher education. This point was made by Betty Vetter, executive director of the Commission on Professionals in Science and Technology:

> . . . [Y]ou can't tell young people you want them to come into the field unless you have something to call it. . . . [I]f you don't have a name for it, I don't know what you are talking about and neither do they. . . .

BOX 2.1 Computer-related Occupational Groups

BUREAU OF LABOR STATISTICS

Current Population Survey [Bureau of the Census]
  Computer systems analyst
  Computer programmer
  Other computer specialist

Dictionary of Occupational Titles
  Systems analysis and programming
    Software engineer
    Computer programmer (alternative titles: applications programmer;
      programmer, business)
    Programmer-analyst (alternative title: applications analyst-
      programmer)
    Programmer, engineering and scientific
    Systems programmer
  Data communications and networks
    Supervisor, network control operators (alternative title: data
      communications technician supervisor)
    Network control operator
    Data communications analyst
  Computer systems user support
    Supervisor, user support analyst (alternative title: help desk
      supervisor)
    User support analyst (alternative titles: customer service representative;
      end user consultant; help desk representative; information center
      specialist; office automation analyst)
  Computer systems technical support
    Computer security coordinator (alternative titles: data security
      coordinator; information security coordinator)
    Data recovery planner (alternative title: disaster recovery coordinator)
    Technical support specialist (alternative titles: project development
      coordinator; technical operations specialist)
    Computer systems hardware analyst (alternative titles: computer
      systems engineer; methods analyst, data processing; information
      processing engineer)
    Quality assurance analyst
    Computer security specialist

Computer-related occupations, not elsewhere classified
  Database administrator
  Database design analyst
  Micro computer support specialist

BOX 2.1—*continued*

Occupational Employment Survey
　　Systems analyst, electronic data processing
　　Computer programmer
　　Computer programmer aide
　　Programmers, numerical, tool, and process control
　　Other computer scientists

NATIONAL SCIENCE FOUNDATION

Classification of Computer Specialists
　　Computer engineer—hardware
　　Computer engineer—software
　　Computer operator, data key entry
　　Computer programmer:
　　　Business/financial
　　　Scientific
　　　Industrial machines/process control
　　　Graphics/art/animation
　　　Other programmers
　　Computer systems analyst
　　Computer scientist except systems analyst (e.g., theorist, researcher,
　　　designer, inventor)
　　Other computer specialists

[W]e need a system that has enough names with which every-body generally agrees—[a system] that can say that an educational institution . . . has [educated] a person with these general competencies and I could count on that as an employer. It would say to the young person, "These are the requirements you will have to take in order to be able to say you have a degree in this field," whatever you call it.

In computing, there appear to be too many names and no agreement about what those names mean.

Need for Better Taxonomies

Many differences in data sets and analyses arise from differences in how subgroups of computing professionals are broken out as elements of a taxonomy used in gathering data. As noted below, NSF collects data from a sample of individuals who have a high probabil-

---

**BOX 2.2   Computing Professional Specialties Derived
from a Sample of North American Leading-edge
Information Systems Divisions, 1991-1992**

Architect/Designer
Business integrator
Business planning consultant
Business process designer
Capacity planning analyst
Customer support analyst
Data administrator
Database analyst/administrator
Data intensive systems specialist
Data security analyst
Emerging-technology specialist
Graphically intensive systems
  specialist
Help desk assistant/technician
Information engineer
LAN system administrator
Network engineer
Network software systems
  specialist

Network systems integrator
Network systems manager
Numerically intensive systems
  specialist
Office systems analyst
Operations support analyst
PC application development analyst
PC support analyst
Project manager
Quality-improvement analyst
Service-level analyst
Skill resource manager
Software engineer
Systems consultant
Systems developer
Systems integrator
Systems maintainer
Systems manager
Systems programmer

SOURCE: Ian Rose, IBR Consulting Services Ltd., Vancouver, B.C.,
Canada.

---

ity of meeting the taxonomic criteria associated with the definition of
a scientist or engineer; NSF reports estimates for the subset of individuals who actually meet these criteria. BLS collects data from a
national survey of U.S. households—the Current Population Survey
administered by the Bureau of the Census—and from a national survey of establishments—the Occupational Employment Survey. The
surveys have different respondents and rely on different taxonomies
in collecting information.

It is not unreasonable for taxonomies to differ because they may
support different goals in collecting data. For example, explained
Alan Fechter, executive director of the National Research Council's
(NRC) Office of Scientific and Engineering Personnel, when the focus
is on supply of talent, the taxonomy will typically refer to embodied

skills such as educational attainment and experience. But when the focus is on demand, the taxonomy will typically refer to occupational characteristics, such as job titles or functional responsibilities.

Workshop participants expressed concern that, regardless of the objectives of a particular data-gathering activity, the known taxonomies of computing professionals appear to have serious shortcomings. For example, confusion and error may arise when different kinds of jobs are grouped within the same category of a given taxonomy. Other difficulties include the fact that a single individual may do work associated with many of the job categories, possibly leading to arbitrary or inconsistent counting, and the tendencies for the taxonomy to assume that work is organized around centralized computing systems or to exclude managers. Overall, workshop participants agreed that job titles alone are poor indicators of what computing professionals do in their jobs, what the skill requirements are, and how the jobs relate to functions performed.

Some of the problems arising from inappropriate taxonomies are reflected in BLS's *Occupational Outlook Handbook*, a guide for career counseling for high school students and others. The *Handbook* covers about 250 occupations but addresses only two categories of computing professionals—programmers and systems analysts. This aggregation into two gross categories was universally decried by workshop participants because it fails to differentiate among a large number of computer-related professional activities valued in the community—such as computer science research, systems management, and systems design—whose practitioners are lumped together with typically lower-skilled individuals. Further, the job titles of "programmer" and "systems analyst" have fallen out of favor in industry, particularly in large firms, with "programmer" increasingly viewed as a relatively low-skill position. BLS recognizes this taxonomic shortcoming and is prepared to add up to three more occupational categories to the *Handbook*. The problem it faces is choosing and defining what those categories should be, a process for which it needs input (and presumably consensus) from the computing professional community.[3]

The level of aggregation, how grossly or finely occupations or jobs are differentiated, is a fundamental issue. As Fechter observed,

> How much you disaggregate these taxonomies to get to subfields or suboccupations or subtitles of jobs depends on how many of them you are dealing with. It is one thing to deal with 10 jobs. The kind of aggregation or disaggregation you talk about with 10 jobs is very different from the kind of aggregation you talk about for 500 jobs or

5,000 jobs or 5 million jobs. . . . It makes no sense to have a very detailed taxonomy to describe three people.

Jane Siegel, of the Empirical Methods Group at Carnegie Mellon University's Software Engineering Institute, underscored the value of even rough estimates of the numbers and characteristics of people engaged primarily in work relating to computer hardware development, computer software development, and systems integration, plus rough estimates of degree production.

> I would like to suggest that for that more senior audience and for the national-level work, keeping it simple is . . . essential. I would be thrilled if in the next major national surveys . . . they did nothing more than simply have a logical, simple structure that broke out people doing computer-related work . . . into those people who work primarily on the hardware side and those people who work primarily on the software side and say something about the folks who integrate it all and make it work together. If I could get even very rough estimates of the degree field and some simple demographics about who those people are and a little bit about their turnover rate and what they do in life, I would have a whole body of knowledge that I think would help a large set of our users.

Toward this end workshop participants agreed on the need for a generally accepted, high-level set of computing professional categories.

Ian Rose, president of IBR Consulting Services Ltd., commented on the challenge of determining how many categories would be ideal, at least for industry: "[M]ost [major] organizations are trying to put together some sort of skills assessment process that works for them. . . . [W]hat you have to do as an individual organization is to determine the number [of job categories] between 15 and infinity, and it will be different for every organization . . . ."

Alan Fechter, echoing Jane Siegel, cautioned that although a moderate level of detail may be valuable for corporate planning, a greater level of aggregation may be appropriate for purposes of national planning and estimation. The steering committee concluded that this issue can be settled only after a thorough analysis has been made of the skills "portfolios" possessed by particular individuals at particular moments in time and those required to perform certain complexes of activities (jobs).

Lack of consistency in available data, as well as the underlying heterogeneity of the group, makes it more difficult to analyze supply and demand for computing professions than for other occupations. Observed Betty Vetter, ". . . I have made comparisons in other fields, and the differences are not significant. . . . [A]lmost everybody seems to agree on what is a Ph.D. in chemistry, what is a Ph.D. in chem[ical] engineering. . . ."

Although other fields evolve, most have been more stationary than computer-related professional fields, and job descriptions and degree titles for them have been more consistent over time. Similarly, the greater acceptance of core competency in other fields allows for less variation in reported counts by survey respondents. Other professions also tend to import fewer people trained in other fields. Noted Jim Voytuk of the NRC, "In . . . for example, physics, one might not . . . go out and hire a biologist. . . ."

Another complicating factor is change in industrial practice. Noted Rose, who specializes in skills assessment and planning, "Many [major corporations] are moving away from job titles and into roles within the organization. So, if you can imagine a skills inventory, it wouldn't call for a business process designer or a systems integrator. It would say, 'business process design function,' and, 'these are the skills you require to be in that function'."

This is not to suggest that there is consistency in industry; Rose observed that one organization may have a position titled "systems integrator" while another may not, although both may require systems integration work. Further complicating the challenge of selecting realistic labels or categories is the need to allow for assessment of changes over time. Commented Robert Kraut, district manager at Bell Communications Research (Bellcore), "[If] you want to know whether the rise of microcomputers has led to a decrease in the need for programmers, you want to have the same definition of 'programmer'." That is, even though the nature and assignment of work may change, a constant metric may be needed in order to measure that change.

Yet more confusion rises from the fact that some computing professional specialties necessarily straddle other fields. Hardware engineering, for example, draws on such disciplines as electrical engineering, mechanical engineering, and solid-state physics, as well as computer science and computer engineering. Software developers, by contrast, face a growing need to understand the area in which their systems will be applied, and they may be substantially educated or trained in that area. This heterogeneous character of computing professional occupations can play havoc with conventional taxonomies. If anything, drawing on people from mixed backgrounds may increase, as the growing complexity of computer systems and their applications increases the value of multidisciplinary collaboration (see discussion of demand in Chapter 3).

THE CURRENT SITUATION

The taxonomic shortcomings described above warn us to treat with caution the available data on computing professionals. Despite such shortcomings, these data can be used to provide rough estimates of the existing situation.

Generally, statistical analyses can be done using data on degrees awarded and/or counts of employed people, which are used to derive direct estimates of levels and trends in supply and demand. Such analyses also use salary levels and rates of employment and unemployment to help assess whether supply and demand are in balance. Other data helpful for assessing future supply and demand include population trends, including shifts in the numbers of entry-level and retirement-age people; trends in the number of high school graduates, undergraduate and graduate enrollments, and undergraduate degrees granted; and attitudes of college freshmen and their intentions to enter different fields. In addition, technology trends are an important factor to consider in examining occupations as technology-dependent as the computing professions.

Sources of data in addition to the federal government's BLS, the NSF, and the National Center for Education Statistics (NCES) include such private and semiprivate organizations as the Engineering Manpower Commission, the Computing Research Association, the College Placement Council, and the American Council of Education/Higher Education Research Institute. A variety of data sets are discussed and compared by Betty Vetter in Appendix A.

Federal data gathering is subject to various limitations. Any changes in field or occupational taxonomy proposed by BLS or NSF for its survey instruments must be reviewed and cleared by the Office of Management and Budget (OMB),[4] the effect of which is to minimize changes. Eileen Collins explained, "What agencies can do is . . . pick a very aggregated, coarse-grained category to survey . . . . They can take a category that is disaggregated and aggregate it further, provided it is possible to add back up to basic categories [approved by OMB]. . . ." Collins also explained that new occupations tend to be added to a taxonomy only after some evidence of their existence has been accumulated: "When enough . . . anomalous people or jobs turn up on a survey . . . you expand . . . the number of categories you have . . . ."

Federal data gathering is also limited with respect to frequency. While some surveys (e.g., the Current Population Survey by the Bureau of the Census) are conducted as often as monthly,[5] most of NSF's surveys are biennial, and BLS's data gathering from the Occupational Employment Survey is further limited by the fact that each group of industries represented is surveyed once every 3 years. Moreover, in each of these cases it may take an additional year and a half for the data to be reported.

Data on Employment

In an attempt to describe the employed human resource base for computer science and technology, data can be used to answer two types of question:

1. Who is working actively in computer science and technology activities? and
2. How are people being used who are formally trained in computer science or computer technology?

Although the two groups of individuals overlap substantially, there is also a substantial area of mutual exclusivity. To a greater extent than in other fields, people actively working in computer science and technology are not necessarily formally trained in these fields; as in other fields, people formally trained in computer science and technology are not necessarily working in this area. The data in Table 2.1 suggest that there are sizable numbers in these mutually exclusive groups.[6]

Because available data are derived from surveys and may have been subject to delays in processing, the most recent data available are often somewhat dated.

The BLS is the best source of information on who is working actively in computer science and technology. Using data collected monthly from the Current Population Survey, the BLS estimates employment in computer-related occupations.

TABLE 2.1 Employed Scientists and Engineers (in Percentages) by Field of Degree and Occupation, 1988

Occupation	Field of Degree		
	Computer Science	Other	Total
Computer specialist	5.8	7.3	13.1
Other	1.7	85.2	86.9
Total	7.5	92.5	100.0

SOURCE: National Science Foundation, Division of Science Resources Studies.

TABLE 2.2   Estimates of the Number of Employed Computing Professionals and Technicians, 1978 and 1988

Source of Data and Occupational Category	Number Employed (in Thousands)	
	1978	1988
National Science Foundation		
Computer specialists, total	177	708
Computer specialists in science or engineering jobs	171	552
Bureau of Labor Statistics[a]		
Systems analysts and computer scientists	182	476
Systems analysts and computer scientists and programmers	337	919

[a]Estimates based on data from the Current Population Survey conducted by the Bureau of the Census.

SOURCE: National Science Foundation, Division of Science Resources Studies, and U.S. Department of Labor, Bureau of Labor Statistics, unpublished tabulations.

Table 2.2 summarizes BLS and NSF estimates of the number of employed computing professionals and technicians for the years 1978 and 1988, the latest year for which NSF data are available. Approximately 1 million people were employed in computer-related occupations that BLS considers professional or technical. Almost 500,000 of these were professionals.[7] Employment in professional occupations overall more than doubled from 1978 to 1988, compared with a growth rate for the entire work force of 20 percent.

The National Science Foundation also supplies information on this human resource pool, basing its estimates on surveys of individuals who meet NSF's definition of a scientist or an engineer. This definition uses as criteria (1) the field and level of degree, (2) occupation, and (3) professional self-identification. Because programmers are considered technicians rather than professionals, NSF generally excludes computer programmers from its estimates, even though computer programming is included as part of the occupational taxonomy of NSF's survey instrument.

The NSF's estimates for non-programmer computing professionals are similar in order of magnitude to those generated by BLS—about 550,000 according to NSF and roughly 475,000 according to

BLS. The trends also match reasonably closely. NSF estimated a slightly faster rate of increase over the period from 1978 to 1988.

The NSF publishes estimates for two sets of employment: total employment and employment in science and engineering activities. Its estimates of the former measure employment of all individuals whom NSF defines as scientists and engineers, regardless of the nature of their work. Its estimates of the latter are restricted to those individuals who meet NSF's definition and who also report that they are working in a science or engineering position.

Although one can conclude from these estimates that approximately 500,000 to 600,000 workers were employed in computer-related professional jobs in 1988 and that employment in these jobs has been growing dramatically, one cannot take comfort from the apparent robustness of these estimates. The significant methodological differences underlying them and possible shortcomings in the taxonomies used provide ample reason to urge caution in their use.

Employment in Academic Institutions

Information on computer scientists and engineers employed in academic institutions is available from BLS, NSF, the Computing Research Association (CRA, which publishes the Taulbee survey), and the Conference Board of the Mathematical Sciences (CBMS). Data generated by CRA are based on information provided by a subset of all institutions: those with graduate programs in computer science leading to the doctorate.[8] Similarly, estimates generated by CBMS are based on information provided by departments of mathematics and departments of computer science. Another source of information is the NRC, which collects information from individuals with doctorates through the Survey of Doctorate Recipients. These data sets are compared in Appendix A.

The BLS data include all individuals who report such employment, regardless of their degree level or institutional affiliation. Thus, unlike other sources, BLS includes in its estimates non-Ph.D.s and individuals employed in community colleges. The NRC data are restricted to individuals who hold the doctorate.

For 1989-1990, the BLS reported 22,000 computer scientists and engineers employed in academic institutions, while the NRC counted about 6,600 academically employed computer science Ph.D.s for the same year.[9] This range in estimates provides a vivid example of the data problems that impede analysis of computing professional labor markets. Factors that may result in the higher BLS number include counts from a broader range of institutions (such as community colleges), from a broader range of disciplines (i.e., individuals with degrees in other fields who teach computer-related courses), and from both Ph.D. and non-Ph.D. holders.

Data on Degree Production

Although degree awards should be among the most reliable and consistent types of data, counts of people with computer science and more or less similar degrees vary significantly (the spectrum of degree programs and their differences are discussed in Chapter 4). The higher the degree level—and the smaller the number of degrees awarded—the greater the agreement on the numbers of individuals with specialized education in computing disciplines.

Vetter (Appendix A) presents three sources of data on bachelor's degrees awarded in computer science—CRA, NCES, and CBMS. The CBMS and CRA data are not examined here since they are derived from subsets of institutions. Estimates generated by NCES are based on information provided by all accredited institutions of higher education. They indicate that roughly 30,000 bachelor's degrees in computer science were granted in 1989 (Table 2.3). This number has

TABLE 2.3 B.S. Computer Science and Computer Engineering Degrees Reported, 1986 to 1990

Year	National Center for Education Statistics	Engineering Manpower Commission[a]
Computer Science		
1985		
1986	42,195	
1987	39,927	
1988	34,896	
1989	30,963	
1990		
Computer Engineering		
1986	2,192	4,999
1987	2,021	5,012
1988	2,115	4,275
1989	2,198	4,398
1990		4,355

[a]EMC surveys only institutions with engineering programs.

SOURCE: Table A.1, Appendix A, "Comparison of Data Sources and Data," Betty M. Vetter.

declined dramatically from its peak of 42,000 in 1986. The dramatic downward trend parallels comparable trends in engineering and mathematics. (See "Encouraging Student Interest" in Chapter 4.)

The Engineering Manpower Commission (EMC), which derives its data from institutions with engineering programs, reports consistently higher numbers of B.S. computer engineering degrees earned than does the NCES (Table 2.3), largely because the EMC numbers include some individuals with degrees in computer science.[10] Taking the NCES estimate as the most comprehensive, B.S. degree production in computer engineering was about 2,200 in 1989, with no trend apparent for the period from 1986 to 1989.

Estimates of the number of doctorates awarded in computer science are generated from data compiled by CRA, NCES, and the NRC. NRC estimates are derived from information provided by the doctoral candidate upon completion of his or her requirements for the degree, whereas CRA and NCES estimates are based on information provided by the institutions. Among sources reporting the number of Ph.D.s awarded, the absolute estimates agree relatively well (Table 2.4). In 1989, Ph.D. production in computer science ranged from 500 to 600, having shown a strong upward trend since 1986. The variation in the annual estimates of the three data sources was less than 100 (in absolute terms), except for 1988, when the CRA estimates showed a larger increase in Ph.D. production than did the NCES and the NRC estimates.

TABLE 2.4 Ph.D. Computer Science and Computer Engineering Degrees Reported, 1986 to 1990

Year	Computer Science			Computer Engineering			
	NCES	NRC	CRA	NCES	NRC	EMC	CRA
1986	344	399	412	56	77	176	
1987	374	450	466	57	61	205	93
1988	428	514	577	77	92	262	167
1989	538	612	625	74	117	277	182
1990		704	734		132	339	173

NOTE: Data from annual and other surveys of the Computing Research Association (CRA), National Center for Education Statistics (NCES), National Research Council (NRC), and Engineering Manpower Commission (EMC).

SOURCE: Table A.2, Appendix A, "Comparison of Data Sources and Data," Betty M. Vetter.

As is the case for its numbers on B.S. degree production, the EMC's numbers for doctorate production in computer engineering are consistently larger than the estimates generated from the other sources and add considerably to the dispersion (Table 2.4). Again, the EMC's numbers are larger because they include some computer science degrees awarded in the engineering schools covered by the EMC survey. Estimates of doctorates produced in computer engineering in 1989 ranged from 74 to 277 (or to 182 if the EMC estimates are excluded).

ISSUES AND CONCLUSIONS

• **Available data are inadequate to guide employers, students, educators, and policymakers.** Both the kinds of data and delays in their publication pose problems. For example, data that are updated every 4 to 5 years will be inconsistent with technology and industry dynamics that change as quickly as those for computing. Because acquiring a comprehensive set of skills data could be prohibitively costly, modest insights might be obtained by collecting and analyzing skills assessments that, according to workshop participants, are currently being undertaken in industry and government.

• **A robust high-level taxonomy of computing professionals is needed.** Currently, data are collected using taxonomies or sets of job titles (see Box 2.1) that are too detailed and too prone to obsolescence as skills needed in real jobs change. For example, "hardware professionals," "software professionals," and "deployment professionals" (responsible for supporting and facilitating the effective use of systems; see Chapter 3) could be developed as gross categories of computing professionals that could have more lasting meaning than do the current large, but inappropriate, sets of occupational titles. However, a high-level taxonomy alone will not provide information on shifting skill requirements; meeting this need requires developing better, more detailed occupational data that take into account shifting technology and industry dynamics.

• **A major need is community agreement on how to label different types of computing professionals and whom to count in each category.** But workshop participants differed on how to implement these changes: academic participants placed a high premium on degree and skill attainment, and industrial and government participants focused more on the nature of the work to be done and the skills applied. This disparity in perspective is not surprising; it reflects the greater challenge evident in industry and government to adapt job descriptions to evolving technology and applications. Thus a number of nonacademic workshop participants referred to skills assessments they have conducted for their employees and clients and emphasized the evolution of job titles and progressions.

• **It is necessary to identify and evaluate changes in portfolios of skills associated with jobs, occupations, and individuals.** Like portfolios containing stocks and bonds, portfolios of skills are subject to change over time in their individual components and in the volume of each component. A job taxonomy is needed that partitions jobs into sets that are equivalent in terms of the skills required. A similar taxonomy for individuals is needed to partition workers into groups with sets of embodied skills that are equivalent. Finally, one must also be able to convert functions required on the job to skills possessed by workers before one can meaningfully assess the strength of the fit between workers and jobs. To properly gauge shifting skill requirements, it is necessary to build on a greater understanding of shifts in technology and industry dynamics.

• **The proposed high-level taxonomy should be related to portfolios of skills, providing a vehicle for tracking shifts in skill requirements that is independent of changing preferences in job titles.** For example, the high-level taxonomy category "software professionals" might include skills that range from simple programming tasks to sophisticated database design or other software development skills. Over time, some skills will diminish in importance as others become more important (see Chapter 3); it is important to track both the details of change and the gross numbers of computing professionals employed in hardware, software, and deployment.

NOTES

1. For example, some workshop participants indicated that computing professionals may show more variability in self-identification than do people in other fields.

2. Another class of workers involved in computer-related activities includes professional users, such as researchers and other professionals who rely heavily on computers to perform their work. For example, a growing number of computational scientists have expertise in both computing and other fields of science. Workshop participants distinguished these professionals from computing professionals by virtue of the fact that they use computers and computer programs as tools—means to an end other than advancing computer science and engineering.

3. A representative of BLS present at the workshop requested such input from participants. As a second step, OSEP and CSTB convened a small meeting in March 1992, attended by representatives of BLS and NSF and individuals who had participated in the October 1991 workshop to explore further the kinds of assistance and input sought by federal statistical agencies. A second small meeting was convened in November 1992 by CRA and attended by representatives of BLS, the Association of Computing Machinery, the Institute of Electrical and Electronic Engineers, CSTB, OSEP, and CRA.

4. OMB is charged with administering the Paperwork Reduction Act, an objective of which is to constrain the volume of information that can be collected via government surveys.

5. Data on the labor force are collected monthly for BLS by the Bureau of the Census through its Current Population Survey. The detailed occupational data derived from this survey are generally reported as annual averages.

6. Because the first computer science degrees were awarded in the late 1960s, it is not surprising to find computer science faculty with degrees from other fields (e.g., mathematics), although their proportion is clearly diminishing. Moreover, according to both data and anecdotal accounts, significant proportions of people engaged in systems development and support do not have degrees in computing disciplines, a condition that is likely to continue (see discussion of employer perspectives in Chapter 3). Robert Kraut noted, "At Bellcore . . . there are 2,500 people who are involved in computer applications development of one sort or another. Half of them don't have a degree in anything related to computer science or computer engineering."

7. Professionals included computer systems analysts and scientists and computer science teachers at the college and university level. Programmers are covered as technical workers (e.g., technicians). Although BLS data differentiate "professionals" from "managers," some managers will be counted as professionals, and certainly the popular conception of computing professionals includes some (technical) managers.

8. CRA's Taulbee survey also includes Canadian schools in its sample. A recent comparison with NRC data indicates that only four U.S. universities awarding Ph.D.s were missing from the CRA data: Clarkson, Memphis State, Nova, and the University of Alabama, Huntsville. A total of eight doctorates were awarded by these institutions—a number so small that one can conclude that differences between CRA and NRC data should be minimal.

9. The reader should be cautioned, however, that academically employed Ph.D.s include more than just tenured or tenure-track faculty. Also included are postdocs and nontenure-track employees supported by soft-money contracts. For example, CRA reports that 8 percent of its estimated academically employed computer scientists and engineers are in such nontenure-track appointments. See Appendix A.

10. In 1991, for example, EMC estimates included 2,177 computer science degree recipients. These individuals were awarded degrees in the engineering schools that report to the EMC.

3

Demand Crosscurrents:
Emerging and Disappearing Jobs

This chapter summarizes the observations of workshop participants on demand for computing professionals. It discusses crosscutting conditions and trends that may affect the overall demand for computing professionals and highlights specific factors that affect demand for individuals in computer-related research, systems and applications development, and deployment.

INTRODUCTION

What employment opportunities exist for computing professionals? The demand for computing professionals varies by specific occupation, as discussed below, but there are general principles that apply to demand for any and all computing professionals, and it is possible to make some general observations about demand for the group as a whole, much as it is possible to discuss demand for health professionals or other multifaceted groups.

The level of demand for any occupational group comes from a combination of employee turnover, replacement hiring, and plans for growth or shrinkage in the volume of employment, among other factors (Box 3.1). Demand can be high not only when employers are expanding, but also when turnover is significant; it can be low when employers are downsizing and also when their work forces are relatively stable.[1] Thus, actions taken by computing and communica-

---

**BOX 3.1   Factors Impinging on Demand
for Computing Professionals**

Factors That Increase Demand

Economic growth
Organizational growth
High turnover
Government technology programs
Increased exports of information
  technology goods and services
Expansion of the user base

Factors That Decrease Demand

Recession
Organizational shrinkage (downsizing)
Low turnover
Defense cutbacks (also, cutbacks in other
  government programs)
Increased imports of information
  technology goods and services

Factors That Are Harder to Quantify

Shift to distributed computing
Shift to more diverse equipment base
Shift in employee mix

---

tions firms to reduce their work forces by tens of thousands (if not more) employees, including computing professionals, and by many major users of computing and communications systems to trim their information systems organizations at the same time, are important indicators of demand, but they represent only parts of the picture.

Demand has qualitative as well as quantitative dimensions. For example, whether or not the total level of demand changes, employers may decide they need more of some kinds of talent and less of others.[2] Thus it is not uncommon to see a company release some employees while it is simultaneously hiring others. John McSorley, human resources manager at Apple Computer, provided a specific illustration in noting that at the time of the workshop (October 1991), Apple had just laid off 600 employees but that at the same time, it had about 720 openings. Demand can also be affected by intangible considerations relating to the desired quality of employees; it is diffi-cult to gauge, for example, the number and types of people who might be employed if employers could find the individuals they think they want.

There is no single monolithic labor market for computing profes-sionals. In particular, computing professionals are not bound to spe-cific industries (unlike, say, miners or aerospace engineers).[3] Pro-ducing, enhancing, advancing, and using computing and communications technologies and applications all create demand for computing pro-fessionals across an ever-broadening range of organizations. As a result, computing professional occupations are growing in relative importance in all sections of the economy. Although the relative growth has been greater in manufacturing, computing professionals are also becoming more prominent in services (Table 3.1). Moreover, within and among industries, different kinds of computing profes-sionals are employed to do the same or similar work, even within the same organization. This variation in hiring patterns and preferences for a given kind of work is among the factors that make it difficult (and potentially misleading) to generalize about the demand for com-puting professionals.

The rapid development and proliferation of computer-based tech-nologies since their emergence in the late 1940s have made comput-ing a growth field over the past 4 decades. Opportunities for com-puting professionals overall have grown rapidly relative to opportunities for workers in other occupations. However, because the computing professional occupations are relatively new and also require special-ized skills, the absolute number of computing professionals has re-mained relatively small—fewer than 1 million in a U.S. work force of over 122 million.[4]

TABLE 3.1 Employed Computer Specialists as a Percentage of Total Employed Work Force in Private Industry, by Sector, 1980 and 1989

	1980	1989
All private industry	2.6%	4.0%
Manufacturing	2.6%	5.3%
Nonmanufacturing	2.7%	3.6%

SOURCE: National Science Board, S&E Indicators, 1991, NSB 91-1, National Science Foundation, Washington, D.C., p. 267.

Moreover, although computing competence is expected to increase in the general population, the number of "true" computing professionals (i.e., individuals who are employed in professional computing fields, as opposed to other professionals who use computer-based tools), like the number of other scientific and engineering personnel, is likely to remain small relative to the labor force as a whole. Table 3.2 gives BLS estimates of civilian employment in 1990 and forecasts of employment in 2005 for nine major occupational groups. Professional specialty occupations, in the BLS taxonomy, included a total of fewer than 16 million individuals in 1990, among them systems analysts and computer scientists, mathematicians, electrical and electronics engineers, physicists and astronomers, college and university faculty, and numerous other professionals. Despite their small number, computing professionals are having a disproportionately large impact as the technologies they develop, produce, and deploy are being used by increasing numbers of people—both in the work force and in other settings.

The fact that computing professionals as a group appear to be relatively well paid suggests that they are not in oversupply. Betty Vetter points out in Appendix A that both starting and continuing salaries for computer scientists are in the top ranks of professional salaries, exceeded by law and business (management) but higher than those for other science- or technology-based occupations.

FACTORS IN THE MACRO ENVIRONMENT AFFECTING DEMAND

While workshop participants expected that overall demand for computing professionals would continue to grow for the foreseeable future, a number of factors suggest that the growth rate is slowing because of short-run and long-run economic conditions (Box 3.2).

The Recession and Slow Recovery

At this writing, the most obvious influence on demand is the recent economic recession together with a subsequent slow recovery, which have depressed demand for employees across the economy. The recession and slow recovery have dampened growth in applications of computing technology and have depressed new business startups, both potential sources of demand for computing professionals. However, the computing sector has continued to grow; sales volume has increased, while prices and margins have fallen.

In general, recessions tend to influence the demand for labor only temporarily. However, what has been unusual about the recent recession is that it was the first to have had a significant negative impact on demand for computing professionals, shattering the perception that these occupations are immune to business cycles.

Elizabeth Nichols, director, Systems and Software Education at IBM Corporation, explained at the workshop that the recession has motivated companies to scrutinize the value they have received from investments in information technology. As a result, they have become more conservative about making new investments in the technology and in the people associated with it. These observations are echoed by reports in trade journals and the business press about the slowdown in orders for new systems, consolidation of information systems (internal application development and support) units, and layoffs by manufacturers and other vendors. The volume of cutbacks has led some observers to speculate that a more fundamental, structural contraction has been taking place, suggesting that many of the jobs eliminated over the past few years will never be restored. Such an inference is qualified, however, by the observations that contraction in the computing sector, per se, has occurred among those segments associated with older approaches to computing and that segments associated with newer approaches, particularly with smaller, distributed systems, have been growing. Also, on the user side, the overhaul of corporate and public computing infrastructure has fed product demand.

Longer-Run Factors

A number of factors led workshop participants to expect slower growth in demand for computing professionals even after the economy has recovered. Some of these factors may contribute to the structural changes alluded to above.

Shifting National Priorities

Joe Kubat noted that the impact of the recession has been amplified by defense cutbacks[5] and by structural consolidation in the financial services and other industries in the northeastern United States, traditionally a region replete with computer specialist job opportunities. Several computer companies based in New England have contracted, merged with others, or gone into bankruptcy. This combination of events may, Kubat suggested, produce significant and enduring declines in demand. Consolidation may also promote a shift in the mix of job opportunities; it is particularly likely to lower demand for

TABLE 3.2   Civilian Employment by Occupation, 1990 and Projected 2005, and Change from 1990 to 2005

Major Occupational Group	Detailed Occupational Group[a]
Executive, administrative, and managerial occupations	
Professional specialty occupations	

	Computer, mathematical, and operations research analysts (including actuaries, statisticians, operations research analysts)
	  Systems analysts and computer scientists
	  Mathematicians and all other mathematical scientists

	Engineers Electrical and electronics engineers

	Physical scientists (including geologists, geophysicists, oceanographers, meteorologists)
	  Chemists
	  Physicists and astronomers

	College and university faculty
Technicians and related support occupations	

	Engineering and science technicians and technologists
	  Electrical and electronics
	  Science and mathematics
	  Computer programmers[b]

Marketing and sales occupations	
Administrative support occupations, including clerical (including 665,000 computer and communication operators)	
Service occupations	
Agriculture, forestry, fishing, and related occupations	
Precision production, craft, and repair (including 530,000 electrical and electronic equipment mechanics)	
Operators, fabricators, and laborers	
TOTAL	

NOTE: Numbers in thousands. Projections for 2005 according to scenario for moderate economic growth developed by the Bureau of Labor Statistics.

[a]Partial listing of selected groups.
[b]Note that the count in this category could include some software engineers as well as lower-level programmers.

Number Employed (Percent of Total)				Change, 1990 to 2005	
1990		2005		Number	Percentage
12,451	(10.2)	15,866	(10.8)	3,415	27.4
15,800	(12.9)	20,907	(14.2)	5,107	32.3
571		987		416	72.9
463		829		366	79.0
22		24		2	9.0
1,519		1,919		400	26.3
426		571		145	34.0
200		241		41	20.5
83		96		13	15.6
20		21		1	5.0
712		846		134	18.8
4,204	(3.4)	5,754	(3.9)	1,550	36.9
1,327		1,640		313	23.5
363		488		125	34.4
246		305		59	24.0
565		882		317	56.1
14,088	(11.5)	17,489	(11.9)	3,401	24.1
21,951	(17.9)	24,835	(16.9)	2,884	13.1
19,204	(15.7)	24,806	(16.9)	5,602	29.2
3,506	(2.9)	3,665	(2.5)	159	4.5
14,124	(11.5)	15,909	(10.8)	1,785	12.6
17,245	(14.1)	17,961	(12.2)	716	4.2
122,573	(100.0)	147,191	(100.0)	24,618	20.1

SOURCE: Adapted from George Silvestri and John Lukasiewicz, "Occupational Employment Projections," *Monthly Labor Review* 114 (11), November 1991, pp. 64-94, Tables 1 and 2.

BOX 3.2   Observations on Demand for Computing Professionals

"My conclusions for the information technology area are that the human resource is growing, but it is growing at a slower rate than it has grown in the past. The new jobs are going to be in the new companies, at the rapidly growing smaller companies, and then the larger companies are going to be focused on the systems integration and systems management problems that have evolved with the rapid growth that they have seen in the past."—*Elizabeth Nichols*

"I think one of the things that we see here is the possibility that we are no longer, in computer science, in a position where the supply falls short of the demand."—*Paul Young*

"[S]upply is not a problem . . . in the commercial business, where the level of intellect may not be as high [as in] research . . . and, therefore, it is possible for us to develop people . . . ."—*Don McLean*

"If what we see in our crystal ball is correct, . . . we would see much less demand for what I will call the low end or what we have traditionally given to entry-level people."—*Linda Pierce*

---

a variety of individuals involved in applications and systems development (although other factors may increase that demand).

Globalization of Markets and Production

The globalization of markets can affect a broad range of employment opportunities, including those for individuals involved in developing computer systems. On the one hand, growth in exports or cross-national ventures, including the opening of new markets (e.g., Eastern Europe), may create new opportunities for computing professionals. On the other hand, the development of overseas markets inevitably implies a growing role for foreign citizens, and international competition in all markets creates pressures for cost containment that could slow growth in U.S. employment.

For example, interest is growing among U.S. firms—both producers and users of computer systems—in employing software developers based in other countries.[6] The motivations for this trend, referred to as "outsourcing," include the lower cost of using software developers overseas and the desire to service foreign markets with local personnel. Noted Linda Pierce, manager, Staff Development and Training at Shell Oil Company: "If you can change the way you package work so that you concentrate on the design component . . . and outsource it overseas, you can get people in India and in Manila and other places . . . with graduate-level degrees . . . who will do this work, too . . . ." Reliance on foreign programmers will affect the mix as well as the level of job opportunities in the United States. Particularly susceptible to displacement are lower-level programming jobs; potential impacts on employment of software developers are uncertain.

Jane Siegel underscored the need to monitor and better understand the offshore outsourcing of software development. She reported that her team's attempt to understand trends in offshore software development started with an examination of half a dozen countries and has grown to address activity in at least 23 countries. Her general observations were reinforced by comments from other participants about their own firms' efforts to use foreign programmers. Nichols contrasted the high levels of demand for computing professionals among developed nations (the United States, Canada, Japan, and Western European nations) with the oversupply of such professionals in certain developing nations, notably India and China: "The estimates I have seen are that there are about 100,000 computer scientists in India, and about 200,000 in China. China has jobs for about 10,000."

Nichols added that international cooperation may affect the whole product cycle, in that a global division of labor may be invoked:[7]

> If we take a look at what the global demand is, what we are going to see are products developed in more than one country. We can already find examples of that today. The research may be done in one country, the development in another. Someone integrates [a product] or puts the components together and assembles it. Then this product can be sold worldwide under multiple logos or brand names and it will have a wide market.

New Economic Activity

Peter Freeman, dean of the College of Computing at Georgia Institute of Technology, observed that consolidation in some sectors could be accompanied by the appearance of new jobs for computing professionals in others, commenting that "[A]ll . . . the activities that corporate America is shedding are going to show up in the economy in other ways." The most obvious shift arises from outsourcing. Increasingly, major computing- and communications-using organizations have been purchasing services such as data processing or software development in lieu of employing workers to undertake them internally. Nichols pointed to systems integration as a growing arena for outsourcing because of its requirements for specialized skills:

> Because of . . . the heterogeneous environment of the many vendors and the communications, . . . systems integration is expected to grow at about 22 percent over the next 5 years. Systems management is expected to grow at about 17 percent. A lot of companies aren't able to do that themselves. So, they are turning to vendors, who have some expertise in how to tie these together. [Such an approach] won't always show up as additional human resources within the [current information systems] community. It will show up as new service companies . . . entering the [market].

The trend toward outsourcing has supported employment growth among a variety of service providers and consulting and contract-labor organizations; workshop participants agreed that it is likely to continue, at least in the near term.

Harder to predict are entirely new forms of economic activity that would stimulate demand for computing professionals. It is relatively easy to identify where contraction is taking place, but harder to forecast new sources of growth, many of which traditionally emerge in small businesses. New businesses demanding computing professionals may arise both within the computer sector and elsewhere in the economy.

CHANGES IN COMPUTER-BASED TECHNOLOGY AND APPLICATIONS AFFECTING DEMAND

Changes in the nature and application of computer-based technologies are having a profound effect on the level and mix of demand for computing professionals. These changes are fundamental to declines in some elements of the computing business and increases in others.

Recent Trends and New Directions

Perhaps the most obvious trend is the shift away from large, centralized computing systems used largely for "crunching" numbers and generating management reports and attended to by teams who took care of the equipment and served as intermediaries between the consumers of computing (the so-called end users) and the computers themselves. The last decade has seen a strong movement to a much larger number of smaller, personalized computing systems that are increasingly interconnected and easier to use. Paralleling this trend is the increase in embedded computing capability in equipment of all types—devices and systems for communications, entertainment, transportation, manufacturing, and so on—and the marriage of computing with telecommunications, video, and other technologies. These trends broaden and enlarge the mix of people who work with computer systems in any capacity.

Employment opportunities reflect the proliferation not only of computing products, but also of applications. Applications are being introduced for virtually every activity undertaken by a business, from marketing (electronic catalogues, point-of-sale data collection) to sales (optical scanning "cash registers," electronic data interchange for order processing, portable systems for field sales representatives) to technical and professional functions (computer-aided design and engineering, knowledge and expert systems for underwriting) to strategic planning (simulation and forecasting systems) and management (labor scheduling, decision support). William Gear, vice president of Computer Science Research at NEC Research Institute Inc., pointed out that in the future there will be even more types of applications. In particular, he suggested, "The collection of data will become increasingly important . . ., as will [their] distribution . . . and publication."

Paul Maritz, vice president for Advanced Operating Systems at Microsoft, explained that the proliferation of applications goes hand in hand with an evolution in software from products best suited to specialized users to products aimed at laypeople (Box 3.3). The magnitude of the potential impact was characterized by Freeman:

> My hypothesis is that very broad and basic application of computer technology and of computer science principles is going to drive a demand curve that is much beyond anything that we currently see. Linear projections aren't going to apply. Here in California, for 30 or 40 years now, freeways have been put out into virgin land [with] about one exit or entrance every two miles, and then houses and industries spring up around those, and then the freeways are overcrowded and there aren't enough exits, and so on. I think the same thing is going to happen in the area of computing.

This view was echoed by Maritz, who referred to the emergence of an information infrastructure with substantial but unknown implications:

> [I]n the next 10 years, the infrastructure will be laid down to . . . bring digital information, initially in the form of movies, into your house, but the fact that you can move data at the rate of gigahertz per second around the world into your home, . . . [and] the implication of that . . . in terms of products, is a fascinating one . . . which whole new companies and industries could be built on.

BOX 3.3 Software Evolution

"[T]he pure software industry, as opposed to the computer industry, has gone through three phases. We went through the first phase in the 1970s, when essentially what we sold were development tools. At that time, if you bought a personal computer 10 years ago, you had to be a programmer . . . because what we supplied with it was a set of development tools and you had to kind of roll your own in the applications.

"Then we developed some broad market applications, spreadsheets, word processors, that appealed to the general people, who were willing to make the investment to become computer literate . . . . We are getting to the point that unless we [expand] that set of people, our industry will become a mature one that grows at 10 percent a year or whatever the economy grows at.

"So, we know we have to make the step out from computer literate people to anyone who is an information consumer. And to do so, we have to rethink how we present computers to people because we can't expect everyone to become an expert on the SQL database language . . . . People just aren't going to do that."—*Paul Maritz*

Leslie Vadasz also addressed the development of the computing infrastructure, in terms of the evolving computer-based environment in the workplace:

> We use computers to do two things. One is to run our business. The other is to report our business . . . . I don't think any of us would have thought of electronic mail as a mission-critical application for our businesses. [But] I think that 5 years from now we will think about it differently, because we will want information at our fingertips and electronic mail will become more of the infrastructure 5 years from now than it has been. So, we really have to understand how such capabilities will be [distributed] in corporate environments to [determine] the need within that environment for various skills.

The emergence of new companies and industries—which will employ computing professionals, among others—is a familiar phenomenon. Over the past 10 years in particular, there has been growth in a variety of computer-based services, ranging, for example, from supply of on-line information and teleprocessing to the expansion of conventional consulting practices into computer applications development.

Implications for Occupational Demand

The changes in computer-based technologies are so large and far-reaching that they will obviously affect employment demand. But just what the impact will be on demand for computing professionals is difficult to forecast. Linda Pierce described an ideal:

> [T]he ideal situation is that there is a core set of skills and education. Then it takes some strategic planning. What kind of technology are you going to be in? What are the directions of those technologies? What are the skill areas that you are likely to need to support those technologies? And then . . . we don't know how to do this, but our objective is to have just-in-time skills.

Over the past 4 decades, new technology has brought a proliferation of computing professional and nonprofessional jobs and occupations. It has included in particular a broadening of professional opportunities—which were focused initially on the creation of computing technology—into applications development and support activities. This broadening has corresponded to the movement of computing systems out of research and into production environments. The emergence of computer scientists and computer engineers has been followed by the emergence of a variety of information systems specialists dedicated to the effective use, management, and adaptation of computing systems.

Comments by workshop participants suggest that it is easier to identify changes in computer-related clerical and administrative support jobs[8] than in professional or technical jobs, which appear to be more fluid and less consistently defined or labeled than other kinds of professional jobs. Participants cited as an example of a newly emerging job in the information systems arena a position titled "local area network (LAN) administrator." People who can fill this position are expected to be in demand for the near future, but the job may also become obsolete with future technology.

According to workshop participants, the nature of likely new technologies and applications suggests that firms and other organizations will make greater investments in areas—and in people who have corresponding skills—such as user interfaces, databases, software development, hardware development, and communications infrastructure, as well as in the integration and the deployment of systems. As Elizabeth Nichols explained, there is growing interest in technologies that enhance the productivity or effectiveness of end users, for example, speech recognition, pen systems, natural language capabilities—some of which require future research as well as development.

Participants agreed that, overall, demand is likely to grow most for skills supporting the development of sophisticated software and the development and deployment of applications. Applications and technologies (notably, computing and communications technologies) will be combined more and more frequently, and the rise of multimedia systems points to broader prospects for technology integration.

Implications for Levels of Skill Required

Technological change is associated with increasing complexity, a general trend suggesting greater demand not only for specific knowledge and skills, but also for increasing breadth and depth of knowledge (about both technologies and applications arenas) as well as greater adaptability. Thus, as noted above, workshop participants expect an increase in the levels of skill required. This situation suggests that requirements for formal education and training may increase, although to date employers have been inconsistent in requiring computer science education (see next section). Nichols, for example, observed that IBM is "purposely trying to enlarge the advanced degree population." Moreover, although it has historically employed significant numbers of software professionals without computer science degrees, IBM performed an analysis of tasks and skills that demonstrated that its entry-level positions now require bachelor's-level training in computer science.

WHAT DO EMPLOYERS WANT?

Differing Views from Industry and Academia

While seeming to agree that more or higher-level skills would be required of computing professionals,[9] workshop participants also indicated that success in working as a computing professional calls for more than technical skills. Participants from industry appeared to place a greater emphasis on the "professional" in computing professional than on the "computing" component. Noted Tora Bikson, senior scientist at the Rand Corporation, when major corporations hire, "[T]echnical competency is definitely not enough. It is probably a minimum condition, and that is true for whatever field they might be recruiting from, but they want the special person." Echoed Gordon Eubanks, president of Symantec, "I don't think that I can remember an individual that failed as a new hire because [he or she] didn't have adequate skills in computer science." This point of view attests to a difference in attitude between academia and industry as to the qualifications sought in computing professionals, and it allows industry employers to meet their demand for computing professionals with relative flexibility by hiring people with a broad range of backgrounds and providing them with appropriate training.

Employers typically focus on getting good, versatile employees— people who work hard and work well with others (Box 3.4). The emphasis on practical skills results in a preference on the part of such companies as Microsoft for recruiting from academic programs that feature work opportunities ("sandwich," "co-op," or work-study programs).[10] While the above comments seemed to apply more to entry-level hiring, similar observations were made with respect to hiring experienced personnel, among whom, workshop participants noted, employers look in particular for evidence of accomplishment.

One reason for this seeming emphasis on generic skills is the rate of technological change. Although they acknowledged it as a common practice, workshop participants from industry pointed to the pitfalls of hiring on a project-by-project basis, an approach that often results in a lack of skills needed for new projects.

Raw talent, though, is not everything: Lucy Suchman, manager of Work Practice and Technology at Xerox Corporation, cautioned that "one problem that arises is that you can have a bunch of people who could turn their hand to anything, but they don't have a clue about what to turn it to."

BOX 3.4   Generic Skills

"Our major challenge is finding those very smart motivated people, who not only come up with great concepts and ideas, but can also inspire the other people around them."—*Paul Maritz*

"[Y]ou need . . . people who are malleable, open to change, able to move with the technology . . . . [P]eople who . . . don't expect to be subject to change will not be in the field for long or they will be 'maxed' out very quickly."—*Joe Kubat*

"[W]hat does it matter if you are going out and hiring someone who is an expert when they graduate in something that will not be around 2 years later? . . . [Y]ou are more interested in . . . someone that is adaptable enough to be taught whatever is the latest thing on the market."—*Barbara Wamsley*

Workshop participants from industry focused on numeracy as a key technical attribute that also is possessed by people trained in a range of disciplines, not just computer science or engineering. At Microsoft, for example, commented Paul Maritz,

> While we focus our efforts on computer science, we don't discriminate against people who don't have a computer science degree, but almost invariably those people do have a numerate degree of some description. They are physicists, mathematicians . . . . We are actually more than willing to make the investment in a smart physicist, for instance, and know that that person is not going to be as effective [at the outset] as somebody who has got 4 years of formal programming training, et cetera. We will take the year that it takes to get the physicist up to speed because we know that we are getting that high-quality individual, which is what really gives us a major impact in our company.

Robert Kraut postulated that this capability to effectively utilize numerate people from a range of backgrounds in software development extends up to the master's level of skill.

Academic computer scientists pointed out that a focus on generic skills may come at a price, since individuals with advanced training in computer science offer a more sophisticated approach to solving technical problems. Observed Marvin Zelkowitz, professor of computer science at the University of Maryland, "[T]he [people] who . . . hire a physicist because programming is easy are taking a very naive view of the intricacies of building a large system. It is more than teaching . . . Fortran or C . . . . There is a lot more involved than that."

Similarly, Peter Freeman captured the two-fold frustration of participants from the research community in commenting on the uncertainty about demand for computer scientists and the apparent ignorance about what advanced training in computer science conveys:

> [T]here is a field of computer science. It is not, anymore, what someone typically picks up with a little bit of self-study. It is something that our typical graduate students go through 4, 5, 6, or maybe more years of rather intensive experiences to obtain. It is a body of knowledge that can be represented in a variety of ways. So, computer scientists at the most advanced level are those people who are pushing the frontiers, who are developing the new technologies. Take object-oriented [programming], . . . something that probably goes back 20 years in terms of the basic concepts. That is what comes out of the basic research that computer scientists do and that, thus, forms the body of knowledge that is computer science. The question in my mind as an educator . . . is how many computer

scientists do we need and how many . . . are going to be pure computer scientists and how many . . . are going to be applications oriented or . . . development oriented?

Unfortunately, due in large part to the problems with data discussed in Chapter 2, it is not possible now to answer Freeman's fundamental question(s).

Employers like Maritz and Eubanks countered that, at least for development of packaged software and mass-market applications, their activities have traditionally centered on implementation of existing technology rather than true innovation, relieving them of a need for depth of education in computer science. However, as the market and products become more sophisticated, greater technical depth will be demanded, because it is needed to achieve product breakthroughs. Thus, workshop participants from both industry and academia suggested that technological evolution may result in greater demand for people with computer science (or related) degrees, at all levels.

The Emergence of Multidisciplinary Teams

Further complicating the interpretation of employer preferences is the tendency of employers to blend computing-related skills with others in multidisciplinary units (Box 3.5). Among the many reasons for this practice is the need for multiple kinds of expertise (e.g., cognitive science, computational science, and so on) to enable development of complex applications that call for understanding of the user environment and insights from other fields.

TRENDS IN DEMAND BY FUNCTION

In addition to examining how the macro environment, technological change, and the preferences of employers can influence demand for computing professionals, workshop participants also discussed demand for computing professionals in particular functions. As pointed out below, career paths and trends in hiring differ for individuals involved in research, in applications and systems development, and in applications and systems deployment (i.e., supporting and facilitating the effective use of systems).

Research

Computer science and computer engineering research is largely the province of individuals holding Ph.D.s. As such, this is the smallest and most specialized segment of the computing professional labor

---

BOX 3.5 Combining Skills

"The people who are writing applications are really going to have to understand the industry and the company that they are writing these applications for."—*Elizabeth Nichols*

"[W]e have a laboratory and within that lab we have an information and computer sciences organization, which is about 150 people, not huge, which has AI (artificial intelligence), advanced software, image processing, and large-scale computational. We are 40 percent bachelor's, 40 percent master's, and about 20 percent Ph.D.s, and we are split about 50/50 between computer science and other degrees." —*Chris Caren*

"In our engineering scientific applications area, we have a . . . new strategy . . . . We want to have about an 80/20 mix; 20 percent of the people doing . . . technical applications work would have a degree in the science area in which that application is being developed. And then 80 percent would have the computer science degree." —*Linda Pierce*

"[T]he experience I have had is that . . . [we need] good communication skills and management that puts together the right mix of people—we have done many jobs for radars, for various internal aspects of missiles, for transportation systems just by pairing the domain person with a good computer scientist . . . . [W]e . . . have more people that do not have CS degrees in large part because we consider ourselves still a hardware laboratory."—*Melissa Smartt*

---

market. However, comments made by workshop participants suggest that the people engaged in computer science and engineering research have more heterogeneous backgrounds than researchers in other fields.

Academic Research

Most basic research in computer science and engineering is undertaken in institutions that offer computer science and engineering Ph.D. programs; applied and some basic research is undertaken in industry.[11] Because the field is young, observed Cornell University's David Gries, professor of computer science, perhaps 50 percent of the faculty in programs that grant Ph.D.s in computer science and engineering have Ph.D.s in other fields. This proportion is expected to shrink as more computer science and engineering Ph.D. holders move into academic positions.

Senior members of the academic computer science and engineering research community have expressed concern about the recent weakness of overall demand in the academic labor market. Historically, it was very easy for a new computer science or engineering Ph.D. recipient to secure a job at a top academic department, but maturation of those departments, declining enrollments, and constraints on research funding have diminished those opportunities.[12] Anecdotal reports indicate that universities are now receiving several hundred applications for posted positions (and may receive tens of applications or more even when positions are not posted), with applicants including new Ph.D. holders, recent Ph.D. holders previously unable to obtain research positions, individuals who fail to get tenure, and individuals from sister fields, such as electrical engineering or mathematics. The result is a crisis in expectations: new Ph.D.s seeking academic employment must reorient themselves to lower-tier universities or to nonresearch institutions, the 4-year (and potentially 2-year) colleges, where openings do exist. New Ph.D.s may also have to consider options in industry or government to a greater extent than previously. Although industry's interest in higher skill levels provides encouragement, Ph.D. preparation traditionally has encouraged students to favor academic employment. A similar situation exists in physics and mathematics, which face added pressure from the new availability of talented individuals from the former Soviet Union.[13]

Another effect of weak demand in the academic labor market is the likely inhibition of the movement of senior computer scientists from industry to academic positions, due to crowding out by younger and less highly paid Ph.D. holders. A diminished flow of personnel from industry to academia would further increase the need for interaction and communication between the two sectors.

Three factors may improve prospects in the academic labor market in the mid-1990s. First, based on demographic projections, the student population is expected to expand at that time.[14] Second, although computer science and engineering faculty are younger than faculty in other sciences and engineering, there will be some retirements.[15] Third, the federal High Performance Computing and Communications (HPCC) program, if fully funded, should begin to have some effect; it is expected to stimulate computer science and engineering research, and thus stimulate Ph.D. production. However, questions arise as to where such new Ph.D.s may be employed. Some senior computer scientists have expressed concern that the HPCC program might increase the supply of Ph.D.s without stimulating corresponding increases in demand.

Some researchers have advocated postdoctoral positions as a means to provide a practical transition from Ph.D. studies to research jobs and to regulate the flow of Ph.D.s into the labor market. Postdoctoral associates are the norm in some fields (e.g., biology), building on traditions in those fields for developing experience, but they have not been common in computer science and engineering.[16]

There was limited discussion of this concept at the workshop. Gries, for example, argued that "a postdoctoral program with 200 more people in it would provide the field with 200 more full-time researchers, which it needs. More importantly, an extra year or 2 of full-time research after the Ph.D. would allow the Ph.D. to mature and gain experience." A postdoctoral program would also provide an opportunity for new researchers to pursue interdisciplinary work, which is of growing interest in academia and especially in industry.

Others, however, argued that the direct impact of labor market conditions is needed to regulate supply and demand for Ph.D.s. According to Zelkowitz, "As academic positions dry up or good ones become harder to find, individuals will make hard choices—a $45,000 assistant professor position at a small 4-year college versus a $25,000 postdoc position at Massachusetts Institute of Technology or Carnegie Mellon University with the chance of a good position there or elsewhere in 2 or 3 years. Different individuals will make different career decisions."

The literature on postdoctoral appointments suggests that they, too, are driven in part by labor market conditions. The number of Ph.D.s holding postdoctoral appointments rises when employment demand is weak and falls when demand is strong, suggesting that such appointments are used to tide new degree recipients over during periods of limited job opportunities.[17] However, if demand remains weak over a long period of time, postdoctoral appointments may simply delay the inevitable, postponing the point at which individuals must make hard choices about their careers. In the biomedical research fields, in which postdoctoral experience is a recognized requirement for obtaining attractive faculty appointments, long postdoctoral apprenticeships are the norm. Moreover, many who have held such apprenticeships eventually wind up in soft-money (nontenured) university positions or in nonacademic employment, generally in industrial or federal laboratories.[18]

Industrial Research

Industry laboratories, like universities, employ people with a mix of backgrounds to do computer science and engineering research. Unlike academic researchers, researchers in industry do not necessarily have Ph.D.s. In industry, the mix seems driven both by the availability of senior computer scientists and engineers and by interest in multidisciplinary projects. Robert Kraut estimated that about 50 percent of the active professional Ph.D.-level computer science researchers at Bellcore lack computer science Ph.D.s and that they "range from mathematically oriented scientists . . . physicists who are doing computer science research now, to people who are not mathematically trained but who are doing research on one of the [Bellcore] core areas, like human-computer interaction." Unlike the more senior faculty at a typical Ph.D.-granting university, explained Kraut, the mix at 9-year-old Bellcore reflects particular decisions on the hiring of new Ph.D.s. These individuals appear to maintain links with both computer science and the other fields in which they are trained, attending two sets of professional meetings, for example.

Paula Stephan, of the Policy Research Center and Department of Economics at Georgia State University, remarked that the flexibility in professional focus at Bellcore described by Kraut is consistent with observations about employed Ph.D. holders overall. Data show "an enormous number of Ph.D.s in science in the United States who say they are working in different areas in different years" when they are surveyed. For example, the Survey of Doctorate Recipients from United States Universities shows that 77 percent of people working as computing professionals (people working in computer science or computer engineering) have degrees in fields other than computer science or computer engineering, while 13 percent of degree holders in computer science or computer engineering are working in occupations other than computing professions. However, Lucy Suchman suggested that individuals with Ph.D.s in computer science might be somewhat less flexible than those whose Ph.D.s were earned in other fields, in part because some employing institutions may not encourage flexibility.

Whereas industrial research in computing has been largely applied (with the exception of some activities in larger companies such as IBM or Digital Equipment Corporation), some new interest in basic research is emerging in companies that believe it is necessary to enhance technology and enlarge the market. This point was made by Paul Maritz of Microsoft, who contended that the broadening of the applications base, which is linked to improvements in the sophistication and ease of use of computer-based technologies, will motivate new research as well as new development activities:

> [F]or the first time in our company, we have recently opened up a pure research department . . . which is what you need . . . if you want to expand your marketplace out into a broader set of people.

. . . [W]e are looking not only for people who have inventive skills—who know how to take established techniques and think up novel applications of those techniques—but also, in very small numbers, for pure research people . . . . We are looking at which computer science programs are preparing theoretical people, whose ideas won't necessarily go into a product immediately.

William Gear and Elizabeth Nichols expressed similar views, also suggesting that there will be a greater demand for higher-level skills.

Expansion into basic research by companies like Microsoft will offset, in part, the diminution of such research efforts at larger companies, such as American Telephone & Telegraph or IBM, which appear to be emphasizing more applied and more focused research in response to market pressures. However, the net effect on demand for researchers is unknown, because of the difficulty in obtaining reliable data on industrial hiring of researchers. Based on their own and their students' experiences, academic researchers in computer science and engineering have expressed concern that industrial research is contracting and that additional small endeavors cannot compensate for contraction in the larger laboratories.

Applications and Systems Development

The development of computing applications and systems dominates the employment of computing professionals in industry, government, and other organizations. It is a heterogeneous activity and, therefore, is difficult to describe and label.

Systems development increasingly revolves around software and its many uses—in individual pieces of equipment, in networks and for integrating diverse components and subsystems into larger systems, for implementing and accessing databases, and for making a variety of tasks easier to do. The number and variety of software types are growing. In particular, development increasingly involves communications technology or applications, due to the spread of distributed systems, the development and broadening application of telecommunications infrastructure, and the blending of computing and communications technologies and systems. Corresponding to the growth in applications, there appears to be a shift among companies from investing in hardware-oriented talent to investing in software-oriented talent. Professional activities include designing, developing, and maintaining (i.e., enhancing and modifying) software; so-called coding, which involves less skill, is done by programmers that are increasingly considered technicians. There is a growing array of computer-based tools to help automate software development processes.

BOX 3.6 Skill Requirements for Development

"We are not in the business of . . . research. We are in the business of building things. As long as we build things with some good methodologies, we don't need a tremendously high level of education and training. So, I don't see a problem even down the road with supply."—*Don McLean*

"[W]e may be less sensitive to the skill levels, as far as computer science goes, because we don't do research and rarely break new ground in computer science. We often break new ground in applying old technology to new problems."—*Gordon Eubanks*

"In developing a spreadsheet or a word processor, you can't really say there is any computer science done there . . . . [I]t . . . was appreciation of what could be done using these techniques, applying them to some problem outside of the traditional computer arena . . . . [I]nventiveness in that sense is different from research."—*Paul Maritz*

Despite its apparent importance, the work of software engineers and what it implies for demand are poorly understood, according to Jane Siegel: "There are very few places where one can get any consensus about what the specific education, background, and/or job performance skills are for someone whom you would call a software engineer. In fact, three states in the country now have legislation on this subject,[19] and it is a growing issue."

Workshop participants from industry emphasized that applications and systems development does not necessarily require advanced training in computer science and engineering (Box 3.6). Nevertheless, an increase in skill requirements for these functions was reported. Gear argued that at least a bachelor's-level education appeared necessary: "I see very little hope for people . . . at the associate level in this area, and even the B.S. is probably minimal. These are the people who are developing the operating systems for the future, the packages, the spreadsheets, the compilers and so on . . . and, of course, the machine designers."

According to Linda Pierce, a primary motivation for using more highly skilled people is the concern about increasing productivity. She noted that computer-aided software engineering (CASE) technology will eliminate "drudgery work" in code generation, reducing demand at the low end, the work traditionally given to entry-level people. With the help of a "technology infrastructure," she posited, "we would see a shift toward the higher end of the technical skills of the people that we bring on board . . . . "

Applications and systems development is driven by the needs and wants of users, and both users and producers of computer systems employ development specialists. This point was made by Chris Caren, vice president of science and technology at Lockheed, who described the fruitful interaction of a small number of trained computing professionals with a larger number of people from other fields who needed computing tools (Box 3.7). The emphasis on use and users encourages the assembly of multidisciplinary development teams.

BOX 3.7   Applications as Drivers of Development

"[A] lot of the real developments [are] user driven . . . . [O]ur company developed a program . . . called CADAM, which is a mechanical design tool. That was done something like 15 years ago and it was done because of the L-1011 [aircraft] program . . . . That [effort] did not involve computer science people. Those were applications-type people, who learned the tricks of the trade.

"In the case of the Stealth aircraft . . . most of [the] programming was done by teams of aerodynamics and electromagnetic people, . . . using new massively parallel machines . . . . [T]hat allows us to . . . not only do better designs, but also [to go] through design optimization . . . . [A] lot of the design optimization [came] over from the computer science domain.

". . . [W]e seeded [our AI efforts] with a few computer science people, but those have been mainly self-taught, again with applications people coming in and being taught the selective methods required . . . to handle their type of problem. In fact, the place where the computer science people have probably made the largest impacts . . . has not really been . . . in computer science. [It] has been in . . . the work that we are doing in advanced software methods . . . . [W]hat we have been pushing there has been not only software reuse, but also automated programming. And, again, that has come from the computer science.

"So, . . . if I were to look at the . . . major developments we have had over the last decade or so . . . it has been highly program-need driven, and that program side of things has been handled more by domain specialists . . . . [O]n the other hand, for the advanced tool [project], as I indicated with reuse, automated programs, and some of the AI stuff, that has come from the computer science [specialists]."
—Chris Caren

And it has promoted the development of computing applications by users and others not originally trained to be computing professionals.

New categories of users are emerging in parallel with more powerful and easier-to-use systems, generating new kinds of applications and new needs for development. Joe Kubat, for example, described a new role in the finance industry for so-called "rocket scientists" with "an R&D-type of . . . technical understanding and expertise," who are highly numerate and may develop and use algorithms for supercomputers and other sophisticated tools to develop new financial products. Maritz generalized by saying, "[T]he fact that computers are much more affordable now makes it more cost-effective to apply analytical techniques to more and more problems."

Applications and Systems Deployment

The proliferation of computer systems and applications has been accompanied by a need for more people to facilitate their deployment. These individuals range from the "applications engineers" and customer support personnel employed by vendors to a range of individuals within system-using organizations, including but not limited to people in information systems departments. Some of the work involves integration of hardware and applications to meet user needs.

This category of computing professional is perhaps the least well understood; it is at least as diverse as the applications and systems development category, and it potentially spans a mix of jobs that may be performed by professionals and/or technicians. In this category, too, skill requirements appear to be increasing. For example, according to an article on vendor support hot lines (which constitute an application of computing and communications technologies to support applications of computing), "Entry requirements are changing to reflect a greater emphasis on service and the increased technical complexity of products . . . ."[20] As a definable group, however, this set of occupations is beginning to coalesce because the need is growing for the tasks involved in applications and systems deployment and because those tasks and the jobs that comprise them are becoming more professionalized. Thus, this is an area of work that bears watching, in the interests of better defining and measuring employment opportunities and trends.

William Gear characterized a range of support functions according to their requirements for education and training:

> In the support area, network administrators, system administrators, people who can provide routine maintenance, the sort of people that a modest-size [company]—by "modest," I mean a company with 10

to 50 people—might need . . . to keep a system running at some level, who know when to take [a piece of equipment] down to the computer repair shop and when to just switch a board, on up through a somewhat higher level [—e.g. a lead systems administrator—] requiring a degree in . . . system administration . . . probably will go through a more traditional educational program, such as computer science, computer engineering, management of information systems . . . on the way to that path.

The need for people skilled in deployment of computer-based systems is expected to grow with the dispersion of intelligent systems and applications across organizations and out of conventional information systems units. As Elizabeth Nichols explained, the dispersion phenomenon may have been launched by people who were technically literate (including scientists and engineers), but increasingly, computer systems are being used by everybody, and notably by people who, unlike pioneering PC users, may not be in a position to do their own troubleshooting. The sheer magnitude of the distribution of equipment to end users will increase the level of system support activity (including training and maintenance), while the increasing sophistication of applications and associated technology may increase both the amount and the quality of system support required as part of deployment (especially training and facilitation).

The need for deployment work is not always recognized and staffed properly within organizations. In particular, the requirements for professional-level skills, training, and judgment may not be recognized up front by employers. In Appendix C Nichols cites the example of the proliferation of LANs and LAN-based applications:

One estimate is that one person is needed to install, upgrade, move equipment, and resolve problems for each 25 workstations or personal computers on a LAN. Very often an undertrained individual in the end-user department is designated to do the work; in this case it is likely that the resource is never counted in the information technology totals. In addition, undertrained personnel make mistakes that often create large problems for information technology personnel to resolve.

Further complicating the assessment of demand for personnel skilled in deployment and other areas is the tendency to outsource some of this work to external service firms. Thus companies may track deployment costs but not actual human resource needs. However, job seekers may find these third-party service providers a significant source of deployment-oriented jobs.

ISSUES AND CONCLUSIONS

• **Crosscurrents are shaping employment opportunities for computing professionals in firms that supply and organizations that use computing technology.** The industrial sector supplying computing technology is metamorphosing: opportunities are declining in the segments based on the centralized computing paradigm but increasing in segments oriented to distributed computing—in firms that develop smaller systems and associated software, networking, and so on. On the user side, the consolidation of the larger firms to achieve economies of scale is offset by the diffusion of computing and communications technology across a widening set of organizations. The general consensus among workshop attendees was that there may be net, moderate growth in employment. But focusing on the averages can obscure the magnitude of the shifts taking place in the mix and the nature of job opportunities for computing professionals.

• **Budget tightening that constrains academic research and the decline of large, central industrial laboratories do not bode well for jobs in computer science and engineering research.** These developments are part of a larger decline in the conventional research environment, and it is not apparent that we have an attractive model for continuing to meet national needs for research relating to computing and communications. Absent other changes, the research component of the job market may decline. Because occupations and functions are not necessarily identical, it is possible that new job opportunities may arise outside of research that can tap the higher skill levels of computer science and engineering Ph.D.s, thus conveying broad economic benefits. But broader use of these individuals is not the same as expansion of the research capability.

• **Required levels of skill appear to be increasing.** Employers represented among workshop participants reported that their skill requirements are increasing in all professional domains—research, applications and systems development, and applications and systems deployment. This circumstance suggests that requirements for formal education and training may increase, although to date nonacademic employers have not consistently demanded formal computer science education.

• **The shift in the mix of skills needed by computing professionals implies a need for education that provides for both flexibility and continuous training.** This circumstance must be recognized by educational institutions, employers, and individuals.

NOTES

1. Measured demand is also sensitive to the level of aggregation of the analysis. Replacement rates arising from turnover will be higher when individual firms are the unit of analysis; they will be lower when industries are examined, since people can move among firms without increasing industry turnover overall.

2. Employer surveys are conducted to assess demand, but they do not always produce reliable information. Generally such information is credible for current employment levels and turnover rates. It is less credible for future employment and qualitative dimensions of demand. Such information has become difficult (and/or expensive) to collect.

3. Even specialists in computer hardware may not remain tied to a narrow set of industries producing computer-based hardware, since such hardware is becoming embedded in a growing range of products.

4. The number of computing professionals may not seem small compared to the number of scientists, engineers, or other technical personnel. For example, unpublished BLS tables for 1991 indicate that there were 95,000 employed mathematicians and mathematical science college and university teachers, 42,000 employed physicists and physics teachers, and 1.8 million employed engineers and engineering teachers (combined).

5. Defense cutbacks, however, do not have a clear-cut effect. For example, explained Jane Siegel, many defense systems have a 20- to 30-year lifetime, creating a demand for individuals to maintain and enhance if not create them. Also, defense systems may be associated with a requirement for hiring only U.S. citizens. For an interesting analysis of the employment implications of the recent dramatic events in Eastern Europe, see Andrew Pollock's "Technology Without Borders Raises Big Questions for U.S.," *New York Times*, January 1, 1992.

6. In the information technology industry the number of new transnational corporate technology alliances has increased from 348 in 1980-1984 to 445 in 1985-1989. The Minnesota Mining and Manufacturing Company now has 2,500 technical employees stationed abroad, triple the number the company had in 1980. See Pollock, "Technology Without Borders Raises Big Questions for U.S.," 1992.

7. For an interesting overview of the issue, see Pollock "Technology Without Borders Raises Big Questions for U.S.," 1992.

8. One example cited by workshop participants was the drop in demand for certain workers associated with mainframe systems, such as "tape hangers" and computer operators; an earlier example might be keypunch operators.

9. Observed Tora Bikson, "I think that what we are seeing is . . . every level shifting up, and there is not a large bunch of low-skill jobs at the bottom level."

10. Paul Maritz explained, "[This approach] really is very effective because we get to see these people in more than just a one hour or a half hour interview and we really find those people who are not only good at interviewing, but really are good at working as well."

11. Note also that some computing-related research can be done in other departments (e.g., interface design in psychology), involving Ph.D.s in both computer science and other fields.

12. See Computer Science and Telecommunications Board, *Computing the Future: A Broader Agenda for Computer Science and Engineering*, National Academy Press, Washington, D.C., 1992.

13. See, for example, American Mathematical Society, *Employment and the U.S. Mathematics Doctorate: Report of the AMS Task Force on Employment*, American Mathematics Society, July, 1992; Jean Kamagai and William Sweet, "Signs of Tighter Job Market

Grow; More than Recession at Work," and "Ph.D.s Fared Worse in 1990 Job Market, Survey Shows," *Physics Today*, March, 1992, pp. 55-58.

14. William G. Bowen and Julie Ann Sosa, *Prospects for Faculty in the Arts and Sciences*, Princeton University Press, Princeton, New Jersey, 1988.

15. Howard R. Bauer and Jack H. Schuster, *American Professors: A National Resource Implied*, Oxford University Press, New York, 1986; and Bowen and Sosa, *Prospects for Faculty in the Arts and Sciences*, 1988.

16. According to unpublished tabulations from the Survey of Doctorate Recipients, Office of Scientific Engineering Personnel, the number of Ph.D.s who go on to hold postdoctoral appointments has been increasing in all fields, however. In the physical sciences, for example, the number rose from 2,500 in 1977 to 3,000 in 1989. The comparable numbers for computer science are 40 and 70.

17. See National Research Council, *Postdoctoral Appointments and Disappointments*, National Academy Press, Washington, D.C., 1990.

18. See National Research Council, *Biomedical and Behavioral Research Scientists: Their Training and Supply*, Committee on Biomedical and Behavioral Research Personnel, Office of Scientific and Engineering Personnel, National Academy Press, Washington, D.C., 1989.

19. The legislation referred to concerns a current debate about whether software engineers should be certified or licensed, especially when they are producing safety-critical software.

20. Alan Radding, "Support: A Hot Line to a Computer Career," *Computerworld*, October 21, 1991, p. 132.

4

Supply: Who Enters the Profession?

This chapter discusses the sources of talent for computing professional jobs, outlines the broad range of educational programs that specialize in developing skills needed by different kinds of computing professionals, and addresses the need to attract and educate a diverse work force for the computing professions.

INTRODUCTION

Where does the talent come from to fill job openings for computing professionals? Computing professionals are those individuals who have acquired the requisite skills by completing appropriate courses of education and training and/or by gaining appropriate experience. They include a large group of individuals who can fill entry-level positions, which typically have the lowest or most general requirements, and a smaller group of individuals who can fill positions requiring more experience or expertise.

Requirements for education and expertise appear most stringent for research positions, where a Ph.D. is typically expected, at least in academia; they are more variable for applications and systems development positions, where employers hire people with varying degrees and levels of education; and they are least stringent for applications and systems deployment positions, where advanced education is not required (but experience is valuable). Accordingly, the talent pool for computing professional jobs is expected to be the smallest for research positions and the greatest for deployment positions. The willingness of employers in industry to train (and retrain) people expands the available talent pool, especially for development and deployment positions. The willingness of citizens of other countries to immigrate (or to work locally for U.S.-owned employers) also expands supply.

Supply is of concern principally as it relates to demand—Are there or will there be enough computing professionals to meet the needs of employers?—and it can be considered from the perspective of current conditions or of anticipated future conditions, which may not be equivalent.

Workshop participants seemed to agree that, given the current economic and public policy context, the total supply of computing professionals today is adequate, although in some specific areas (e.g., systems research, systems integration, certain kinds of software development), especially in those with requirements for very specialized applications knowledge or experience, it is not. Representatives from industry differed in their outlook on supply, depending in part on the amount and kinds of hiring they contemplated. One factor that may contribute to an increase in the available talent pool is the slowdown in defense spending, which is expected to free up computing professionals as well as other scientific and technical personnel. Paul Stevens, manager of Corporate Software Initiatives at Hughes Aircraft Company, noted that this effect on human resources may be disproportionate, since commercial projects tend to use fewer people than comparably sized defense projects.

Workshop participants seemed to agree that supply may not be adequate as we approach the 21st century, for two reasons. First, as discussed in Chapter 3, skill (and education) requirements appear to be increasing. Leslie Vadasz emphasized this trend as a source of concern and a motivator for action: "[E]mployees of the future will need more . . . baseline education, . . . higher than it was 10 . . . or 20 . . . or 30 years ago . . . ."

Second, too few people appear to be pursuing education and training relevant to work as a computing professional. Betty Vetter underscored the difficulties posed by changing current and future prospects: "One of the worst problems of . . . supply and demand is [seen] in the situation we are in now, . . . where current supply exceeds demand and most of us expect future . . . demand to exceed supply." Vetter also noted that even today, computing professionals are relatively well paid, a sign that they are valued.

DEGREE PROGRAMS

At the core of the talent pool of computing professionals are those individuals who have earned degrees in computer science or a related field. Although in many fields (e.g., physics, chemistry, and various branches of engineering) degree holders constitute a clear majority of those working in the field, in the computing professions a large proportion of employed individuals have degrees in other fields. In part, this unique characteristic of computing professionals reflects the relative newness of degree programs in this field and is typical of emerging disciplines. Over time, as programs in computer science proliferate on campuses, the proportion of individuals who work as computing professionals but have degrees in other fields can be expected to decline.

Currently, however, degree production in the field is a weaker indicator of the supply of computing professionals than of the supply of professionals in other fields. Further complicating an assessment of supply based on degree production is the variety of programs offering a degree related to computer science. Before considering the numbers of degrees awarded, it is useful to understand the kinds of degrees being counted. Education and training for computing professional jobs as a group can be gained in 2-year programs (although in general, computing professional jobs require at least a 4-year course of education), baccalaureate programs, master's programs, and doctoral programs.

The range of programs is described in a paper (Appendix B) prepared for the workshop by A. Joseph Turner, a professor in the Department of Computer Science at Clemson University, and summarized below. Turner notes that "a program's title in itself doesn't tell you much about what is in the program, and there is a lack of standardization." As Turner explains, attention to degree options (as opposed to separate degree titles) in electrical engineering and possibly other sister disciplines might result in an even greater number and variety of programs than those he lists. Turner's presentation underscores the problems that arise in attempting to categorize and analyze available information on degree production.

Two-Year Programs

Two-year programs, of which there are several hundred in the United States, are oriented toward producing candidates for entry-level jobs, including people who want to switch fields. They focus more on acquisition of specific skills than on the general principles and concepts that characterize 4-year college and university programs. Two-year programs range from combinations of two or three courses in programming languages to more substantial curricula; they may focus on the use of specific applications (e.g., word processing, spreadsheets, or computer-aided design) or on rudimentary programming.[1] The scope and rigor of these programs are such that, absent other skills, their graduates are typically considered candidates only for lower-level deployment (e.g., technical support) and technician (as opposed to professional) positions.

Baccalaureate Programs

Most people who pursue an education in computing complete a baccalaureate program. Baccalaureate programs related to computing, which offer from 6 to 15 courses of varying quality and rigor over 4 years, have a range of names such as computer engineering, computer science and engineering, computer science, computer information systems, information science, information systems, management information systems, and management of information systems.

In terms of the types of graduates they aim to produce, baccalaureate programs can be grouped loosely in three categories—liberal arts, professional, and basic science. Liberal arts programs tend to be broad and little oriented to development of specific skills; professional programs tend to focus on development of skills (production of professionals); and basic science programs, much like 4-year programs in the physical sciences, are broader than professional programs and provide a foundation for graduate study.

Because of a lack of consistency, the distinction between bachelor of science (B.S.) and bachelor of arts (B.A.) degrees is meaningless in computer-related fields. Recognizing that program and degree titles are not used consistently, it is nevertheless possible to categorize bachelor's programs according to their substantive focus, along a spectrum that includes a hardware (engineering) orientation at one end, a science orientation in the middle, and a management-of-information-systems orientation at the other end. Curriculum guidelines are produced by the Association for Computing Machinery; the Accreditation Board for Engineering and Technology, for engineering degrees; the Computer Science Accreditation Board, for computer science degrees; and, for some 2- and 4-year professional and management-oriented programs, by the Data Processing Management Association (see also "Education Curricula" in Chapter 5).

Discussions at the workshop concentrated on skills and curricula most closely associated with computer science or engineering; less was said about information systems or information science, in part because of the makeup of the group. While both information systems and information science programs are primarily concerned with computing, they have other emphases. Information systems programs focus on management concerns and on the use of computing and communications systems in the business environment; information science programs focus on the use of technology to organize, store, and retrieve information, with a secondary emphasis on cognitive and decision science. Graduates of these programs are oriented to deployment and some development activities. By contrast, computer science and computer engineering programs are distinguished by their focus on computer science and computer engineering foundations and concepts. Graduates of these programs are oriented to development and, when they pursue further education, to research.

Computer science and computer engineering programs overlap substantially, with computer engineering programs putting more emphasis on hardware—although today, many hardware designers tend to come from electrical engineering rather than computer engineering programs. The engineering orientation of computer engineers equips them well for applications work (e.g., in manufacturing). Turner notes that, like other engineering programs, computer engineering programs tend to be well defined.

Master's Programs

Master's programs produce graduates who are hired for applications and systems development jobs and sometimes industrial research jobs. Turner estimates (Appendix B) that more than 300 departments offer master's degrees in computer science, about 95 in information science, about 72 in information systems, about 33 in management information systems, and about 40 in computer engineering. Master's programs have varying requirements, ranging from course work only to course work plus a project or paper or thesis, and may also offer specialization in such areas as telecommunications, decision support systems, and artificial intelligence.

Master's programs can be either traditional science programs or professional programs. In computer science, master's programs have tended to be intermediate steps en route to a Ph.D. They are science and research oriented, providing more education and skills than a bachelor's degree but no particular training relevant to development activity in industry. As a result, and in reaction to feedback from industry, there has been some discussion in the community about the need for a terminal professional master's degree in computer science. By contrast, prominent among master's programs are those in the areas of information systems and management of information systems, the latter sometimes related to M.B.A. programs. According to Turner, information systems programs may have significant computing elements (including software development) as well as business elements, whereas management of information systems programs tend to focus more on business and management issues.

Two new types of master's programs tend not to be captured in aggregate statistics: master's programs aimed at producing software engineers, of which there are now 15 to 20 in the United States, and master's programs in computational science (the application of computing to large-scale scientific problems), of which there are now a handful.

Doctoral Programs

Doctoral programs in computer science and computer engineering are tracked in detail in the Taulbee survey (conducted by the Computing Research Association), as discussed in Chapter 2. There are fewer than 200 such programs. Although counting the computer science and computer engineering Ph.D.s they produce is relatively easy, it remains the case that the contents of those programs, and therefore the quality and competence of their graduates, are not consistent.[2] Less is known about doctoral programs in the related areas of information science and information systems, which are not covered by the Taulbee survey.

Within the academic computer science and engineering community, the optimal rate of production of Ph.D.s has become a subject of debate. Central to that debate are expectations for 1,000 Ph.D.s per year established by the federal High Performance Computing and Communications program, which establishes research and human resources directions for computer science, computer engineering, and computational science. Workshop discussions raised some concern that targets are apparently being based on, at best, imperfect forecasts of demand. As noted in Chapter 3, limited industrial requirements for Ph.D.s and uncertain prospects for research funding create uncertainty about optimal Ph.D. production levels.[3]

One issue discussed at the workshop was how the mix of ages of people in the field might affect the supply of computing professionals. Betty Vetter noted that as a group, computer science Ph.D.s are considerably younger than engineering, physical sciences, or mathematics Ph.D.s. As a result, computer science will not face the problem expected in other fields between 1995 and 2000, when a large number of retirements are expected.[4] Vetter cited the American Council on Education's *Campus Trends 1991*, which observed that its membership, which includes most academic institutions, highlighted computer science as having significant faculty shortages today, but also indicated in response to a follow-up question ("And do you expect this to be better or worse in five years and at about what level do you expect it?") that they expected faculty shortages to be reduced in computer science, and only in computer science.[5] The evidence on age distributions and the institutional responses reported by the American Council on Education do not support the hypothesis of future shortages of computer science doctorates as strongly as does comparable evidence for doctorates in other fields. Also, anecdotal evidence from mid-1992 suggests that there is a surplus of candidates for faculty positions, at least for those at upper-tier schools.

FUTURE SUPPLY: PIPELINE OR AQUIFER

The supply of computing professionals for the future depends primarily on the supply of people capable of and interested in pursuing relevant bachelor's degree programs; the supply of future computer science and engineering researchers depends further on the number of people capable of and interested in pursuing higher degrees, especially Ph.D.s. Adequate supply is a concern even when demand is expected to grow slowly or be flat, both because people will leave the field and have to be replaced and because when there are more qualified people, there will be better odds of achieving a good fit between individuals and jobs.

The future supply of computing and other professionals is often discussed in terms of a "pipeline," the numbers of people at earlier stages of education with appropriate interests, aptitudes, and prerequisite course work. Workshop participants expressed discomfort with the pipeline metaphor. They suggested that supply might be described instead in terms of an *aquifer*. Observed Robert Weatherall, director of placement at the Massachusetts Institute of Technology,

> We are heading into a desert—we have a lack of a skilled population at many levels. What we need to do is to keep the aquifers filled. . . . Once there are really bright people at the college level and then people getting master's degrees, once . . . the water level is really high, then Ph.D.s will flow.

The aquifer model also allows for infusions of talent at different points (e.g., people who switch fields and/or return to school as adults), whereas the pipeline, which focuses on what happens over time to children with quantitative aptitude as they proceed through their schooling years, seems to emphasize the process of attrition and a single source for talent. Although workshop participants did not analyze the issue explicitly, a number of comments pointed to the variety of ways in which people have entered computing fields indirectly or at later points in their careers (see, for example, "Experienced Workers," below). Thus, they pointed to the importance of "in-migration" or transfers as a historic source of supply, although their comments about rising skill requirements suggested that opportunities for in-migration might diminish over time or at least involve more formal education or training as formal programs producing computer science graduates continue to diffuse through the higher education system.

Encouraging Student Interest

Workshop participants expressed strong concern that the number of young people preparing for computing professional jobs is inadequate. To a limited extent, the field may be suffering from a tarnished image: a positive image is fundamental to attracting and retaining talented people in the computing professions. Although these occupations as a group are perceived to be in strong demand and to be well paid, workshop participants suggested that the work of computing professionals may be poorly understood. Moreover, the value of some subspecialties may be underappreciated, even within computer technology firms or academic computer science departments. Participants from industry observed that companies may compartmentalize computing professional activities, limiting apparent advancement opportunities (although some companies offer strong technical-professional career paths). Participants from academia noted that work on large complex systems, which is of special value to industry, typically does not fit well with academic reward structures and advancement opportunities. As a result of these conditions, talented people may choose alternatives to professional computing careers.

The problem of attracting students to computing professions was discussed by workshop participants in the context of the more general problems of declining interest in scientific and engineering fields of study and weak preparation in math and science in the kindergarten through high-school period. This point was made by Tora Bikson, who referenced her research on career opportunities:[6]

> [P]eople in corporations, . . . foresee a very short supply of computer scientists and engineers . . . in the United States, especially, . . . 5 to 10 years out, and their perception is that this is so because stu-

dents aren't being attracted into mathematics and sciences at the grade school and the high school level.

Vetter noted that enrollments at the bachelor's level in all of the numerate fields (those requiring a significant background in mathematics) have been dropping since 1986. Brenda Wallace, program analyst at the Bureau of Labor Statistics, described data from the National Center for Education Statistics (NCES) that show that bachelor's degrees in computer science and engineering peaked in 1985-1986 and have declined subsequently. Moreover, the rate of growth and the subsequent decline were greater for bachelor's degrees than for all other degrees in these fields. Participants associated with universities augmented this general observation with comments on their own experiences with declining enrollments in computer science programs over the past couple of years, declines that follow a long period of growth. There is little in the literature that rigorously attempts to disentangle the many factors that might be fueling the decline. Possible reasons for the recent downward trend in computer science degrees include inadequate student appreciation of the rigorous requirements for the degree, expectations that job opportunities are poor, greater attraction of other professional careers, and so on.

Declines at the bachelor's level are part of a larger process of attrition, as William Lupton, professor in the Department of Mathematics and Computer Science at Morgan State University, noted in the context of discussing minority interest:

> There are several leakage points along the way [and] we have to get students through each one of these points. The reason there are so few minority Ph.D.s in . . . computer science is that there are few master's degree holders, and the reason there are few master's degree holders is that there are few baccalaureate degree holders. And it goes right on down the line.

While Lupton's statement is appropriate to the production of doctorates in computer science, the concept introduced by Weatherall of an aquifer, rather than a pipeline, allows for the possibility of a flow of talent from other fields—whether into Ph.D. programs or into jobs for computer professionals that require a doctorate.

Workshop participants reinforced the notion that interest in computing professional occupations, as in others in science and technology, must begin at an early age, especially for underrepresented groups (Box 4.1).

Richard Tapia, professor of mathematical sciences at Rice University, was one of several participants to emphasize the important role of elementary teachers and the need to devote energy to improving

---

BOX 4.1 Starting Early

"The pipeline has to start long before the student arrives at your front door at the baccalaureate level. If the student hasn't been prepared prior to his arrival at college, he is not going to make it in science and engineering. Therefore, we have to address the pipeline earlier in the student's development . . . [starting] about the fourth or fifth grade. . . . [W]e need to impress upon these students at an early age that science . . . is a good thing to pursue. If we wait until a student has a choice to take a science . . . or a math . . . course and . . . one of his peers says, 'oh, don't take that math course; it is tough . . .,' that plants a seed that will germinate and grow and cause the student to avoid science or math . . . . [W]e need to impress upon students . . . that science . . . is a good thing to pursue . . . before they [decide] . . . that they don't want to pursue math and science.

"Further, there is a problem with students getting the proper counseling and guidance, not only from their teachers, their counselors, but . . . from the parents . . . as well. Part of the pipeline issue may be a program to . . . train the elementary school teachers and counselors so that they are sensitive to this and bring the message to the students at an early point, that it is a good thing to do, to tackle that math or that science course. . . .

"What we have to do is provide whatever stimuli [are needed] at the early point so that we can maintain these students in the program over the extended period of time. That will require not only training, but monitoring and mentoring as well."—*William Lupton*

---

their skills: "[E]lementary school teachers . . . love to teach and love kids, but . . . they all have math anxiety. No doubt about it. They don't know this, and they transfer it to their students." Concern was also expressed about inadequate preparation in high schools for college programs requiring significant quantitative achievement or rigor.

Although on a national basis relatively few children have significant exposure to computers through their schools, workshop participants challenged conventional wisdom by asserting that precollege programs often appear to discourage rather than encourage interest in computer science and engineering. Although this topic was not discussed at length, possible reasons identified include poorly designed programs and poorly prepared teachers. There was also some speculation that, as computing systems become more common, the technology may lose its allure while the work involved in meeting future requirements may become harder.

Experienced Workers

While typical discussions of supply focus on attracting and educating children and very young adults (candidates for entry-level jobs), older individuals may also provide a source of talent. Although, as a new field, computer science was originally populated only by people trained in other fields, the potential to increase supply today by retraining is often undervalued, according to some workshop participants. Paula Stephan, for example, spoke of the changing demographics of college students:

> [O]ne of the great paradoxes in recent years in education has been why we continue to have more students in colleges and universities, despite the baby bust generation coming of age. The answer to that is that . . . the huge growth in the United States [has been in] students of non-traditional age. That means that [many of] the people who are knocking at the door for higher education are in their late twenties and their mid-thirties . . . .

Tora Bikson reinforced Stephan's comments by drawing on her interviews with employers and professionals. She has found that increasing numbers of people want to be able to move between work and education, although many universities do not encourage this:

> It used to be that there were two kinds of students, those who get a degree and go to work and those who get a degree and then go into graduate school . . . [but] there [are] more and more cases of students who would like to work for a while after their baccalaureate degree, to get a sense of what the career perspective looks like, sometimes just to earn money for a change or to escape the pressures of school and into the pressures of work. But very many times the traditional faculty doesn't look positively on someone who has polluted [his or her] career this way.

Workshop participants from industry provided another perspective on late entrants to the field in discussing efforts to shift personnel from one type of work to another. Leslie Vadasz observed that corporate restructuring is changing demand in ways that will be difficult to interpret or even to capture in data:

> Corporate America is under tremendous pressure to downsize, restructure . . . . [This situation] is going to create all kinds of misleading . . . data for anybody who is looking at a pipeline, because . . . [they] won't see demand. Yet, at the same time, demand is there in a different way . . . in retraining your own people or in terms of . . . new skills . . . .

According to John McSorley, Apple finds it can retrain only about 30 percent of the people whose positions it eliminates, turning outside for new people to fill the majority of its openings. Elizabeth Nichols noted that IBM has had success in training mechanical engineers, among others, for computing professional positions.

One reason for historically limited levels of retraining in industry has been the relatively high levels of mobility among computing professionals. Commenting on the West Coast labor market, for example, Paul Stevens noted that computing professionals tend to be more mobile than engineers. McSorley suggested that today, software engineers continue to be particularly mobile, as evidenced by an attrition rate four times that of hardware engineers at Apple. William Gear suggested that the mobility of U.S. computer scientists may be a potential area of American vulnerability:

> I view this mobility issue as perhaps one of the most serious problems facing American industry. I see there too [much] mobility, . . . causing industry to have little incentive to train people. The emphasis on the individual in American culture, particularly in research, I think is one of the things that perhaps puts us behind the competition in [Japan]. . . .
>
> An American researcher sees his or her resume as basically the only employment card for the future. In Japan, employees see service to the company as their guarantee to the future.

Marvin Zelkowitz echoed McSorley and Gear in noting that mobility is high for some specialties: "In computer sciences, . . . good people in more practical areas are really hard to find at almost any level, and there is extreme mobility among artificial intelligence (AI) systems, software engineering, and that type faculty, mostly out of the university system."

Even in industry, good people may be lost as technical resources in instances where rewards are perceived as greater in such nontechnical jobs as management. Accordingly, some companies have experimented for years with dual career paths, although the greatest success tends to be within the computer industry; major users (e.g., banks or insurance companies) appear to have more difficulty establishing technical career paths that offer sufficiently rewarding upper levels.

PROMOTING DIVERSITY

The total supply of computing professionals is only one part of the picture; another important part is the composition of the supply in terms of how well different sociodemographic groups are represented. Noting that enrollments for women appear to be dropping faster than the average and remain very low for non-Asian minorities, Betty Vetter summed up multiple data sets as follows:

> There are a lot of major differences in these data, but all the data show three general trends . . . an increasing and quite high proportion of foreign nationals, . . . small and not increasing numbers and percentages of women, and an infinitesimal number of African Americans and Hispanics. Asians . . . seem to be either appropriately represented relative to their 3 percent of the population or overrepresented . . . .[7]

Equality of Opportunity

Discussions at the workshop underscored the concern about equality of opportunity and breadth of participation in computing professional occupations, both of which are considered essential for the health and growth of the field. Paul Young, associate dean of engineering at the University of Washington, set the stage in his overview comments for the discussion of these issues:

> I think we all understand that . . . if the United States wants to maintain a good technical work force, changing demographics will force us to have more women and more minorities in technical positions . . . . But aside from the issue of the demographic needs . . . science and engineering are areas that give economic advancement to people, and what is currently happening is excluding a major part of the American population. . . .
>
> The record of computer science, while it looked good a few years ago, is, if anything, getting worse, at least with respect to women, and it has never been good with respect to underrepresented minorities. . . .
>
> One of the things I was struck by as I listened to members of our panel . . . is that some of the factors that seem to keep women and minorities from computer science probably also account for the general decline in interest in computer science across all populations . . . .

Richard Tapia reflected on his experiences in encouraging Hispanic student interest and emphasized that the true problem is one of female and minority participation in science and engineering as a whole:

> The problem we are talking about is certainly not unique to computer science. In mathematical sciences, [there are] 1 percent Hispanics and African Americans. So, it is really [a problem for all of] science and engineering. And the problem should be attacked from that point of view, not that this is something that computer science has failed on. . . .

> [T]he population of women in the United States stays constant, [while] representation in science and engineering [as a whole] is slowly going up. With minorities, the population is growing extremely rapidly, and yet, their representation is at best staying constant . . . . Of course, I would not argue that it is [a crisis] for the profession—I think we have seen a history in mathematics and computer science that we import solutions. We don't have to turn to our local population. On the other hand, I think it is extremely important that we realize that this extremely large, expanding population is outside of all science and technology, and that this is bad for the country.

Workshop participants were concerned that current labor market conditions undercut shortage as a major motivation for encouraging broader participation, although they expected that scarcity may be a problem in the future. It should be noted, however, that even a stable population allows for changes in the mix of participants—even without growth, increasing diversity can be achieved without actively taking jobs away from white males. This is so because some amount of voluntary turnover (e.g., retirements and resignations) is normal, and the vacancies that result provide opportunities to increase representation from previously underrepresented groups. But workshop participants did not foresee a steady-state situation; rather, they anticipated slow growth, and growth can increase the number of opportunities available for all kinds of candidates.

In addition to the growth argued for, there are other compelling reasons for efforts to improve the participation of underrepresented groups. Argued Young, "You can't have groups that are permanently shut out, and you can't get real participation . . . until you get enough people in. It seems to me that we have to continue to make that argument on . . . moral grounds."

There are also arguments for promoting diversity that are based on doing good science. For example, women and underrepresented minorities bring to science perspectives that push research efforts in directions in which they might not otherwise go.[8]

Paula Stephan noted the political dimension: "If you think about the importance of science to our culture and . . . to growth in the U.S. economy, the idea of evolving into the 21st century and being a society in which certain groups are almost virtually [without] representation . . . creates enormous political problems . . . ."

A final argument for promoting diversity is based on the underemployment of talent implied by the low levels of participation of these groups. This underemployment represents a cost to society that could be reduced by altering the demographic mix of computing

professionals, even if total employment remains the same. Econo-
mists attribute this cost to market failure arising from the effects of
discriminatory behavior.[9]

And Robert Weatherall characterized the need for broader participation as economic:

> [I]t is a question of the skills infrastructure. Compared to Japan,
> . . . Germany, . . . and Singapore, this country has a lack of skills
> across the population at different levels . . . . [E]ducation disciplines
> are the vehicle for [providing general] skills—mathematical skills,
> writing skills, social skills . . . and [learning] computer science is a
> good . . . educational vehicle. So is mathematics. So is physics. . . .
> [A]ll [should] contribute to the skills infrastructure.

Minorities

The problem of limited participation in computing professional
jobs is particularly stark for African Americans, who typically account for zero to two computer science or engineering Ph.D.s awarded
per year, with eight the annual maximum ever recorded in the Taulbee
survey (in 1990-1991).[10]   Throughout the period from 1970 to 1991,
these numbers translated to either 0 percent or 1 percent of computer
science Ph.D.s awarded each year. Correspondingly, a negligible number
of African American faculty work at Ph.D.-granting institutions covered by the Taulbee survey. William Lupton, also then president of
the Association of Departments of Computer Science and Computer
Engineering at Minority Institutions, noted that undergraduate interest in computer science and engineering has remained relatively high
in colleges and universities historically attended by African Americans, although there, too, there was a surge in the mid-1980s. Alan
Fechter speculated that some of this numerical strength may have
come from a reorganization and renaming of programs previously
associated with mathematics or other sister disciplines and since designated as computer science and engineering programs. Peter Freeman noted that the 1980s also saw increased activities by major companies to stimulate interest among and provide financial support for
minority youth:

> AT&T, for example, and IBM have very strong programs . . . provid-
> ing scholarships, . . . making regular visits to those campuses, send-
> ing people, sending equipment, and then guaranteeing jobs when
> those people get out . . . . [T]he really bright ones should be going
> on in the graduate pipeline, and we are seeing very explicit evi-
> dence that they are so attracted by the salary in going to work at
> Bell Labs, Bellcore, or IBM that they don't go on to graduate school.
> . . . But . . . to me, that is [also] a positive outcome . . . .

Lupton echoed Freeman's ambivalence, noting that some corporate recruitment programs also provide support for further education. Joseph Turner pointed out that diversion of talented minority students from Ph.D. programs translates into a smaller pool of candidates for faculty positions and a virtual absence of role models for future minority students.

Richard Tapia noted that underrepresented groups fall into two categories: obviously talented women and minority graduate students are courted and may have a choice of sources of financial support or good jobs in industry, whereas the larger pool of potential talent remains undeveloped. Wade Ellis, professor in the Mathematics Department at West Valley College, noted that the problem of the larger pool of minority students is compounded by the fact that people of limited means tend to go to schools with limited resources.

The limited participation of Hispanics in computing programs presents some of the same challenges as participation of African Americans. Within Ph.D.-granting institutions covered by the Taulbee survey, Hispanics compose 1 to 2 percent of Ph.D.s produced and faculty employed in computer science and computer engineering. Understanding the Hispanic situation is complicated, Tapia explained, by the fact that published data tend to overlook the heterogeneity of Hispanics. Although over half of U.S. Hispanics consist of Mexican Americans and Puerto Ricans, most of the people counted as Hispanics in science and engineering appear to be from Central America—a minority within a minority—and the majority of Hispanics have negligible participation in science and engineering.

Women

In Ph.D. programs in computing, the overall representation of women is low when judged by the fact that they represent one-half of the talent pool, but high when judged by their representation in other fields of physical science or engineering: women tend to receive less than 15 percent of computer science and engineering Ph.D.s, having earned 12 percent in 1990-1991 in the Taulbee-surveyed institutions;[11] other sources of data cited by Betty Vetter show the same order of magnitude. Among Ph.D.-granting programs covered by the Taulbee survey, women compose 8 percent of computer science faculty and 4 percent of computer engineering faculty totals, including only 4 to 5 percent of full professors. Although women share the problem of underrepresentation with minorities, increasing the participation of women overall is expected to require a somewhat different set of solutions than increasing participation of minorities.

Among minority students, women appear to outperform men. According to Vetter,

> Female African American students do far better relative to African American males, than do female students in any other racial or ethnic group relative to the men within that same group. In engineering, for example, women make up 30 percent of the engineering baccalaureates awarded to African Americans and only 15 percent, approximately, in all the other fields. But in computer science, the African Americans have [had] a really big climb in the last years . . . .

Tapia indicated that among Hispanics, women also sought computing and mathematics degrees more actively than men.

However, Vetter pointed out that the prominence of foreign students in science and engineering programs tends to work against growth in the participation of women: "The inclusion of more and more foreign students is detrimental to the [measured participation] of women . . . in any field at the Ph.D. level . . . because foreign students will include far fewer women than American students will." Vetter also noted that language and cultural differences between foreign and American students appear to discourage American students, who often have difficulty with foreign-born teaching assistants.

While there is substantial anecdotal evidence of corporate programs to stimulate the interest of women and minorities in science and engineering, Tapia contended that Ph.D.-producing universities do not present as welcoming an environment, something evidenced by the paucity of women and minority faculty in those institutions. Lucy Suchman reinforced the concern about the environment in Ph.D. programs, which she suggested is particularly hostile toward women as "polluting" elements.

> [W]hat actually happens to people when they encounter the institutional realities . . . ? That is what makes people drop out and that is what makes the barriers higher as you go up. For women, they come in great numbers and as we look up the management hierarchy, they get harder and harder to find . . . . [Female graduate students in computer science] . . . get demoralized in absolutely astounding ways. . . . [T]he conditions . . . they encounter [are] . . . those of a very tightly knit club . . . which they are polluting. As a consequence, they suddenly find themselves extremely marginalized and taking it all on as a personal shortcoming, rather than as a limit of the situation.

Paul Maritz, as an employer, noted the difficulties he faced as a recruiter in search of women and minority candidates at top-tier schools.

Robert Kraut observed that one way to involve more women is to redefine the field in a broader manner, to embrace the multidisciplinary nature of some of the current challenges. Suchman echoed this argument, suggesting that new models should be considered.

> Computer science in Denmark is a . . . very formal discipline, . . . traditional, . . . narrowly defined, but [increasingly] there are . . . departments of information that are co-located with departments of computer science, and they have very high representation of women. Basically, what they are about is a much more complex assembly of activities, including a lot of attention to the intrinsic requirements of the technology . . . . Those kinds of programs . . . really redefine what the whole enterprise is about in a way that, at least for the women . . . I have talked to, . . . [makes it] a much more attractive field to get involved in.

Paul Young revisited related concerns in reporting on his conversation during the workshop with Essie Lev, counselor, Information and Computer Science at the University of California at Irvine (UCI). Based on her experience with UCI's computer science department, Lev said, "One of the reasons we are losing students in general, and women and minorities in particular, is that we have lost a sense of passion and a sense of social relevance about what we do." Historically, women (and perhaps to a lesser extent minorities) have sought out fields, such as biology and the social sciences, that emphasize social relevance and teamwork. By emphasizing those areas of computer science and computer engineering that most require those qualities, it may be possible to attract more women (and minorities) to computing professions.

FOREIGN-BORN CITIZENS

Workshop participants indicated that an important question is whether the pipeline for computing professionals is becoming global. Although they recommended that the question be studied more systematically, indirectly they appeared to answer the question affirmatively.

Computing professionals of foreign citizenship appear to be a significant presence within the United States. They are key elements in staffing some research and educational institutions and are prominent among student populations, especially at the graduate schools. For example, NRC data indicate that 54 percent of computer science Ph.D.s from U.S. universities in 1991 were earned by foreign citizens.[12] Moreover, foreign students are often better prepared than American students. A large number of the foreign-born students stay in the United States after they complete their educations and become part of the domestic talent pool.

At the same time, the growing stock of foreign computing professionals and the globalization of various markets mean that computing professionals located abroad are becoming more attractive to U.S. employers, as discussed in Chapter 3. Moreover, advances in communications systems and cheaper communications facilitate the use of remote staff, whose contributions can be transmitted quickly and easily. Immigration may also provide a significant amount of talent to our domestic pool. The contributions of foreign-born scientific and technical personnel to the country have been recognized in recent immigration reforms, intended to facilitate recruitment and retention of foreign scientists and engineers in the United States.

ISSUES AND CONCLUSIONS

• **Greater and more effective efforts are needed to attract a more diverse group of people to computing professions to more closely reflect the demographic makeup of the country and assure survival of the field.** In particular, women and non-Asian minorities ought to be encouraged to choose and continue in professions in computing fields.

• **Although differences in educational curricula across institutions are consistent with the rich and dynamic nature of the field, an excessive degree of variation may be counterproductive.** For those who are interested in a computing career, the educational arena presents an array of choices so broad as to be confusing. Virtually every dimension, from labeling of programs to content, seems to vary, in every class of program. Perhaps improvements in taxonomies for data collection (see Chapter 2) can serve as a guide to educational institutions and students, helping to focus the skill development process.

• **While computing professional jobs are likely to continue to attract people from other fields, increasing skill requirements may call for more fundamental education in computer science and engineering than was needed in the past.** However, the trend toward greater cross-disciplinary interaction in addressing problems in computing and other domains might serve to fuel further in-migration. How different trends will balance out is unclear at this time.

• **Because skill needs are changing rapidly in industry, educational institutions need to produce graduates with the ability for and commitment to continuing future learning.** In theory, these are consequences of good programs of basic education; in practice, it is not clear that these objectives are being met.

NOTES

1. A set of new curriculum recommendations is under development by a committee of the Association for Computing Machinery, a professional society. This group has classified 2-year programs into five categories, four of which are relevant here, including computing and engineering technology (hardware-oriented programs), computing and information processing (information systems-type courses), computing science (more computer science oriented), and computer support services (including functions like computer operation).

2. This problem is not unique to computer science and computer engineering, but many have the impression that the situation is more serious in computer science and computer engineering.

3. See Computer Science and Telecommunications Board, *Computing the Future: A Broader Agenda for Computer Science and Engineering,* National Academy Press, Washington, D.C., 1992, for a discussion of research trends and needs. As that report notes, the opportunities for Ph.D.s will be greater where individuals have broader views of what constitutes interesting and legitimate research activity. Although employers may specify a requirement for Ph.D.-level education relatively infrequently, Ph.D. holders have skills that could be applied beneficially in nonresearch activities, including development. However, as Elizabeth Nichols observed, employers sometimes have difficulty merging Ph.D. holders in development roles.

4. Retirements and deaths are increasing in Ph.D.-granting institutions. The Taulbee survey reported 35 such separations in 1990-1991, more than twice the level of the previous year, a level that had also exceeded that of earlier years.

5. Elaine El-Khawas, *Campus Trends,* American Council on Education (ACE) Reports, Number 81, ACE, Washington, D.C., July, 1991, pp. 10-12, 36. The statistics refer to all institutions of higher education, including community colleges. If the analysis is restricted to doctorate-granting institutions, an increasing proportion of the respondents expect future shortages. This finding applies to each of the individual fields covered in this survey, including computer science.

6. T.K. Bikson and S.L. Law, *Meeting the Human Resource Needs for Success in a Global Economy,* College Placement Council, Bethlehem, Pa., 1992.

7. Vetter noted that the discrepancies in statistics about Asians suggest that some surveys may count Asian Americans with foreign nationals, and some, appropriately, may not.

8. Evelyn R. Keller, *Reflections on Gender and Science,* Yale University Press, New Haven, Conn., 1990.

9. See, for example, Gary Becker, *The Economics of Discrimination,* University of Chicago Press, Chicago, 1971.

10. David Gries and Dorothy Marsh, "The 1990-91 Taulbee Survey Report: The Computing Research Association's Survey on the Production and Employment of Ph.D.s and Faculty in Computer Science and Engineering," Department of Computer Science, Cornell University, Ithaca, N.Y., December 1991.

11. These numbers include women of multiple nationalities, not just U.S. citizens.

12. Data from annual and other surveys of the National Research Council's Office of Scientific and Engineering Personnel.

5

Training, Retraining, and More Retraining

This chapter discusses the implications of likely shifts in demand for computing professionals and of current trends in their supply for education and training programs. It builds on discussions in earlier chapters about continuing shifts in the nature and mix of computing professional jobs and the need for a strong basic education that will prepare individuals for further training over time.

OVERVIEW

A principal mechanism for adjusting the supply of people to better fit job opportunities is investment in education and training. As discussed in Chapter 3, the number and mix of job opportunities for computer specialists are changing; as discussed in Chapter 4, education relevant to computer specialists is available in a wide variety of programs, institutions, and delivery mechanisms. Not surprisingly, discussions at the workshop revealed differences in perspectives between educators (primarily computer scientists) and employers in industry, but they served to highlight the principal issues for education and training of computing professionals.

In introducing the discussion of education and training at the workshop, Linda Pierce voiced the goal of reaching "a consensus around a core set of knowledge and skills" to support future career paths. Discussions at the workshop suggested that although there were areas of agreement, the community lacks consensus regarding career paths and core knowledge or skills, in part because of the widely shared view that the field—and therefore any related career path—is so dynamic. Workshop discussions centered on two themes: the appropriateness of the education of entry-level personnel, and the need for periodic retraining to keep personnel in the labor force up to date.

Pierce spoke for many when she remarked that, with technology changing in cycles as short as two and a half years, "the ability to forecast and prepare for this future skill mix will certainly grow more complex in the future." William Gear sketched out how the evolution of the field may translate into rising educational requirements for those engaged in computer-based technology development:

> Down at the very lowest level, you might even find people with associate degrees helping some very small company in some minor way with modifications of spreadsheet software . . . . In the future we are going to . . . see those people go through a [4-year] degree program that is heavy in the application area, probably not a major in computer science or management information systems, whatever it is called, but a minor to develop the necessary computational computer science skills and a major in the primary area of application.

Gear suggested that the trend toward embedding more and more computer devices or systems into other equipment or systems will result in significant new skill requirements and potential problems in meeting them.

The unresolved question is whether skill needs will be met in the classroom or on the job. Education and training are not preordained outcomes; they present choices for multiple parties—individual students, educators, and employers—whose outlooks often differ considerably. Ian Rose articulated the tensions between the interests of the individual in career development planning (including personal choices in education, training, and jobs to nurture his or her own career as a computing professional) and the interests of the employing organization (for which the individual's needs are secondary) in skills assessment and succession planning. James Williams, chair of the Department of Information Science at the University of Pittsburgh, pointed to the need for career counseling: "[People] need some kind of help because they don't have time to pay attention to all the nuances of what is happening in industry. They are busy doing their work." Participants from industry echoed Williams' assessment that planning for both education and training involves shared responsibilities.

Yet several participants suggested that today's computing professionals are not always as flexible and able to move with the technology as employers would like. Thus the challenge is how best to prepare people, through education and training, for the kinds of change the field may require of its practitioners and to inculcate the capability to be adaptable in response to these changes.

Part of the problem, which affects many scientific and technical occupations, may reflect fundamental difficulties in harmonizing technical and managerial perspectives. According to Robert Weatherall, the initial education and work experience of engineers, and, by extension, of other segments of the computing professional community, may sow the seeds of discontent among engineers. He cited studies about the frequency with which engineers quit the field and go into management, often via M.B.A. programs. Weatherall suggested that one way to alleviate this problem is for engineering programs to encompass management issues, thereby helping to prepare engineers to progress into management and helping them to understand the relationship of their technical work to the operation of the organization as a whole. Participants also noted that in some organizations, efforts have been made to develop attractive technical career paths that parallel managerial career paths, but existing efforts do not solve the larger problem. Alan Fechter speculated that making technical career paths more rewarding would become a more urgent need over the next 10 or 15 years "because it is going to be harder for firms to recruit at the bottom. So, [employers] are going to have to think more carefully about how to utilize the resources they already have in-house."

EDUCATION CURRICULA

Going hand in hand with a lack of consensus on how the field and its practitioners should be labeled (see Chapter 2) was a lack of consensus on how accreditation might be used as a means of standardizing computer science programs and on what the core requirements should be for such programs.

With respect to accreditation and standardization, Marvin Zelkowitz contrasted the conditions in academic computer science with the more stable and predictable conditions in such fields as physics or chemistry: "When I am asked what is the core of computer science, my comment is that it is whatever the computer science faculty want to teach." Similarly, Peter Freeman argued that "all of us have a strong responsibility to continue to push the formation of a core computer science discipline, and that is only going to happen by the continued healthy production of Ph.D.s, in some sense almost forcing them into the market."

These observations were reinforced by the comments of Joseph Turner and others about the evolution of criteria for departmental accreditation. Although such criteria exist and seem to be becoming more widely adopted, accreditation is not a major driver for the top-tier, Ph.D.-producing departments. One reason may be the current lack of consensus about the ideal content for the field; Zelkowitz, for example, complained that the accreditation criteria were too focused on basic computer science. Another concern expressed was that accreditation requirements do not keep pace with the fast-moving field.

With respect to the nature of the core curriculum, workshop participants debated the degree to which programs should be vocationally oriented. Those discussions reflected the divergent perspectives that exist between individuals in the academic research community and those in industry. The major area of disagreement concerned how much colleges and universities can or should do to teach either work-process skills or specific techniques. Zelkowitz acknowledged that educators have had difficulty with applications-related material, although he cautioned against an overly vocational approach. He suggested that while computer science departments started out with a "practical" orientation, they were likely to become theoretical over time, for two reasons. First, individuals oriented more toward applied work are more mobile, because they have more job opportunities; second, universities are not conducive to the undertaking of lengthy, large-scale experimental projects.

Freeman observed, "There are certain specialties—systems software, systems building more generally—[for which] we basically cannot find good people either in quality or quantity . . . . And, yet, those are precisely the areas in which industry wants the most training among our students." Speaking from industry, Robert Kraut remarked that "In Bellcore's research organization, there are a large number of Ph.D.s in computer science, but there are very few of the sort that Bellcore is looking for, which are the systems researchers." A shift toward theory would weaken the fit between the education supplied by colleges and universities and the skill sets preferred by industry.

Zelkowitz and other participants also noted that universities traditionally have not devoted much effort to specific issues of concern to industry—project management, teamwork, cost estimation, evaluation of alternative designs, risk management, for example—because those issues are crowded out by other items in the curriculum and because typical computer science faculty are not sufficiently knowledgeable about them.

David Gries summed up the frustration of computer science faculty with requests from industry for more practical and/or specific training. He observed to the industrial attendees, "You people want computer science to do more and more"; and he noted that undergraduate programs have only so much capacity for content. Ultimately, workshop participants agreed that the principal function of colleges and universities is to provide a foundation (including concepts, problem-solving skills, and so on). As William Lupton explained:

> [T]his gets at the heart of what we in the universities are all about in the first place. We teach students how to think. We teach students to . . . solve problems, using the theories and principles of the discipline and apply them to different challenges in the workplace. If the challenge changes, then they apply those principles again. The jobs may change, the tasks may change, but the paradigms don't change that often. If [there are] requirements for a change of paradigm, then they can go back and get retrained for it. I think what is missing [from] this discussion . . . is that when we develop students, we have developed a person that thinks and . . . can apply that thought process to the particular job. If that job changes, the person should be able to reapply those principles again and still be effective.

Gries argued that some of the limits on program content reflect fundamental faculty limitations:

> [O]ne of the problems that we face in the field is that over half of the people who are doing the teaching at this point in all the colleges and universities and community colleges do not have a computer science background themselves. That is a real problem because of all the significant advances that are happening these days. We have object-oriented programming, functional programming—[but] most of the people teaching don't know about these things . . . . [T]here is a real . . . need for continuing education for computer science teachers.

Similarly, Gries pointed out that computer science departments are not likely to address organizational and management issues (e.g., cost-estimation and teamwork) through case studies because "that requires the teacher to know something about those topics and that is not the case for most computer science faculty members." Paul Young contended that, overall, universities are responsive, if not rapidly so.

Freeman, in fact, addressed the dangers of too quick a response from academia:

> [A]s educators, we have a responsibility to lead, not just to follow, the marketplace demand . . . . [T]he danger is that if we listen only

to the marketplace, of course, what we hear is, "We want more people that know object-oriented programming." Well, that is great, but that is not what you are going to need 5 years from now. I think all of us here know that and none of us know what you are going to need in corporate America or industrial America 10 years from now. Yet, the product that we produce in universities presumably has a useful lifetime of 40 years. So what the universities must continue to do is to produce that long-range product.

Freeman also stressed the need for more interdisciplinary education: "[W]e need a new educational product that has . . . combined . . . parts of [computer science, electrical engineering, and business/management] . . . . I look at that as a third generation of computer science, what we are calling computing, which is a combination of the core computer science and some other discipline."

Among industrial participants, Don McLean argued that broader perspectives in general, drawing from liberal arts, would be valuable. Paul Maritz, acknowledging some of the limits of what academia can do in providing work-related training, suggested that more specific skills may be the province of master's and doctoral programs:

> The university can't give the student big-systems experience. They can't put together a 100-person project that runs for 3 years, which is what you have to do . . . . [I]ndustry has to supply that side of the picture. What you want [from] the schools is training in analytic thought, in good work habits, in curiosity. These are the types of things that you would like to see come [from] the undergraduate institutions . . . . [T]he postgraduate institution is where we can look for more specific skills, somebody who really has been trained in depth in computer graphics, for instance, or in computer linguistics. That is where you can look for people who understand modern principles and techniques that can be applied.

Robert Weatherall observed that most of the communication between employers and universities comes from big companies, a factor that might bias the message.

Finally, Leslie Vadasz urged greater and more thoughtful communication between industry and academia:

> Some of this discussion reminds me of problems in dealing with our customers. In a high-technology business, there is a difference between what a customer wants and what he needs. Customers generally can tell you their "wants" based on their experience. But new technology can create capabilities beyond their "wants," and you need to evaluate if they really "need" it. There is a similar interface between universities and employers. We in the industry can probably state our "wants" on the basis of our most recent or current

experiences. But can we define what future skills we need? Maybe yes; maybe no.

I believe that it behooves the supplier—in this case the universities—to understand what future issues their customers—in this case the employers—will face, so that they can better supply what their customers really need. This is where industry-university dialogue has to continue. We don't go out to hire a Ph.D. As Paul [Maritz] said, we hire on the basis of certain accomplishments . . . . It is very difficult to specify demand in a very fast-moving field like this.

TRAINING

Training, per se, is largely a concern for computing professionals engaged in applications and systems development and possibly deployment. Training is generally provided or paid for by employers.[1] In addition to on-the-job training, sources include workshops, seminars, conferences, and programs offered by universities and professional training organizations. Speaking from their experience, workshop participants described a labor market in which employers, especially large firms, are investing more and more in training people to meet their particular needs (Box 5.1); this practice allows them to focus on specific skills when making hiring decisions, as discussed in Chapter 3.

Workshop participants agreed that training is an ongoing concern for computing professionals because of the dynamic evolution of computer science and technology. As a result, they suggested, computing professionals should be educated—and employed—with an orientation toward lifelong learning and periodic retraining. James Williams identified four principal categories for retraining: literacy or basic identification of things and processes; concepts, "where you need to understand some relationships and you need to understand how [something] fits into some structures or some forecast"; knowledge, "where you really need to understand how to solve problems, how to do analysis and synthesis and evaluation of a particular area"; and skills acquisition, the "how-to" category.

It was no surprise that the issue of how much retraining should be provided and how frequent retraining should be was not resolved by workshop participants. Barbara Wamsley suggested that training would be a constant, recurrent activity: "When you know you are dealing with an occupation with a half-life of 2 to 5 years, you are going to have to train these people in 2 years anyway if you are going to keep the same quality that you hired."

Ian Rose noted that, along with changes in skill requirements

---

BOX 5.1 Employer-based Training

"[Y]ou simply can't afford not to be in the internal training business. Whether internal training means having internal training staff or tapping the commercial suppliers or, indeed, the local colleges and universities, we simply have to be in the business of training, and I would suggest more and more as change increases."—*Don McLean*

"It is interesting to me, sitting in a careers office, to see firms like Arthur Andersen, Andersen Consulting, Electronic Data Systems, the big brokerage firms like Morgan Stanley, and then the big insurance companies . . . . [T]hey seem to think that the thing to do is look for the bright folk and then have a very elaborate training program, so they will know exactly what they should be learning and doing within [for example] the insurance company."—*Robert Weatherall*

"What we hear also from industry is that they think the universities should do what they do well, which is to provide more basic science and broader intellectual support, but not try to teach people how to do a very specific product-oriented task, which might well turn out to be out of date. That it is an appropriate division of labor: that universities should do education, and that companies should then do the training."—*Tora Bikson*

---

associated with changes in technology, concurrent changes are occurring in organizational structure (e.g., organizational flattening, outsourcing, or downsizing) that are altering the opportunities for advancement and professional growth among personnel in industry. Linda Pierce also enumerated managerial concerns that complement concerns about technological change: product delivery needs, business savvy, ease of use of technology and applications, ability to work in teams, more formality in product research and development, higher-quality expectations, and so on. These concerns should motivate new directions in education and training. Rose pointed out that individuals may not keep pace with how technological and organizational shifts affect advancement opportunities. Thus, they may develop unrealistic aspirations. At the same time, contended Peter Freeman, managers may not be sufficiently knowledgeable about the options and implications of new technology to make the best training decisions about either technology or jobs.

Both individuals and managers are struggling to forecast needs and opportunities in areas that involve computing; the uncertainty and dynamism of the time imply that flexibility and an ability to shift to new skills and responsibilities are especially valuable. Pierce presented the employer's perspective on the need for flexibility: "[O]ne thing we have to expect is that these people understand that they have chosen a field that is going to have rapid change in it . . . and they have to be committed to learning as a lifelong thing, if they are part of this kind of work."

Participants from industry acknowledged that some people would feel more pressure to change in their skills than others. This variation in the training needs of industrial employees reflects, in part, the need to support or maintain systems throughout their life cycles. For example, Chris Caren contended,

> I don't [believe] that everyone is involved in this change process. We've got systems that we have had for 20 years that are written in [the 1950s-vintage programming language] COBOL. They will probably be around for another 20 or 30 years if we can't afford to change to anything else . . . . [P]eople that are involved in the maintenance of those [systems] . . . —a vast number of people involved in our computer applications—hopefully are going to get some retraining. But they wouldn't need to have retraining. Then there are others in the very mobile world of new projects . . . [who must] have the retooling, the reskilling, and so on. That is where you put your more flexible people. So, this renewal process probably only really needs to be done for a percentage, and I don't know what it is—30 percent, 40 percent of your work force.

Workshop participants acknowledged that individuals differed in their receptiveness toward retraining. Williams noted that incentives, including financial support or promotional opportunities, can help to encourage retraining. John McSorley described how some 70 percent of those whose skills are no longer needed at Apple are unwilling or unable to be retrained, and as a result they leave the company. Shelby Stewman, professor of sociology and demography at Carnegie Mellon University, speculated that applications skills are neither as transferable nor as malleable as most might expect. He observed that workshop participants and people he has interviewed in industry have indicated that it is difficult to transfer people across system and application areas; it is often easier to hire someone new with the appropriate skills. Participants were, in the one and one-half days of the workshop, unable to articulate more than a general sense that needs for frequent retraining will continue in the future and may even expand, given expected trends in new technologies.

ISSUES AND CONCLUSIONS

• **Changes in skill requirements will be a way of life for computing professionals.** This conclusion arose from discussions of education and training as well as supply and demand.

• **Frequent retraining may be necessary to meet shifting needs for skills.** The educational system can support this requirement both by producing graduates with broad and flexible skills and by contributing to more effective and more available retraining through interactions with industry.

• **Corporations must reconcile themselves to the financial and organizational commitments implied by continuous shifts in skill requirements.** Changes in skill requirements may result in some dislocation for individual employees. But rather than simply replacing employees, in the long run it may be more effective to update their technical skills while leveraging all of the other skills and capabilities required of employees to make organizations effective.

NOTE

1. As discussed in Chapter 4, some entry-level training is also provided in 2-year and other short-term educational institutions, but those programs generally are oriented toward computer users or associated production and clerical personnel rather than computing professionals.

6

Conclusion and Next Steps

The vitality of the computing enterprise and its components—the academic disciplines, the industries, and the specialized professional occupations—and its growth and contributions to the economy make supply and demand for computing professionals a matter of national interest. That enterprise will continue to be dynamic, although slower rates of growth are anticipated by those in the field as we approach the 21st century. Overall, significant changes are likely in the mix of computing professional skills required by employers, and there is an expectation that computing professionals will need to have increasingly stronger technical skills. It is also widely believed that a technically skilled labor force will remain essential to securing a competitive position in a global economy. But discussions at the workshop underscored how difficult it is to really measure, and therefore evaluate, the kinds and numbers of computing professionals who are employed today, could be employed, are being educated or trained, or may be needed in the future. The discussions at the Computer Science and Telecommunications Board (CSTB) and Office of Scientific and Engineering Personnel (OSEP) workshop on these and other issues were far-ranging and led to the findings and conclusions outlined in this chapter. Almost by definition, they laid a foundation for further, more thoroughgoing consideration of a range of issues identified as important for the field and the country. A clear consensus of participants was reached on the observation that their discussions should be considered the beginning of an ongoing dialogue.[1]

This chapter recapitulates the key conclusions developed in Chapters 2 through 5 on data and taxonomy, demand, supply, and training. The conclusions are complemented by pointers to next steps for addressing issues more directly.

ACKNOWLEDGING EVOLVING DEMAND

Changes in computer and communications technology, combined with changes in the economy—in the structure, growth patterns, and geographic reach of industries—are altering the demand for computing professionals. Demand is further complicated by a growing internationalization of the computing professional work force.

- **Crosscurrents are shaping employment opportunities for computing professionals in firms that supply and organizations that use computing technology.** The industrial sector supplying computing technology is metamorphosing: opportunities are declining in the segments based on the centralized computing paradigm but increasing in segments oriented to distributed computing—in firms that develop smaller systems and associated software, networking, and so on. On the user side, the consolidation of larger firms to achieve economies of scale is offset by the diffusion of computing and communications technology across a widening set of organizations. The general consensus among workshop attendees was that there may be net, moderate growth in employment. But focusing on the averages can obscure the magnitude of the shifts taking place in the mix and the nature of job opportunities for computing professionals.
- **Budget tightening that constrains academic research and the decline of large, central industrial laboratories do not bode well for jobs in computer science and engineering research.** These developments are part of a larger decline in the conventional research environment, and it is not apparent that we have an attractive model for continuing to meet national needs for research relating to computing and communications. Absent other changes, the research component of the job market may decline. Because occupations and functions are not necessarily identical, it is possible that new job opportunities may arise outside of research that can tap the higher skill levels of computer science and engineering Ph.D.s, thus conveying broad economic benefits. But broader use of these individuals is not the same as expansion of the research capability.
- **Required levels of skill appear to be increasing.** Employers represented among workshop participants reported that their skill requirements are increasing in all professional domains—research,

applications and systems development, and applications and systems deployment. This circumstance suggests that requirements for formal education and training may increase, although to date nonacademic employers have not consistently demanded formal computer science education.

Next Steps: Better information is needed to monitor and understand changes in demand for computing professionals. One approach may involve a systematic analysis of advertisements for computing professional jobs; the content of such advertisements may suggest shifts in the demand for skills as well as the evolution of job titles and hierarchies. To understand the direction and general magnitude of changes in skill requirements, decisionmakers need not only data, but also an understanding of relevant business and technical trends. Federal statistical programs will be a necessary part of the process; professional and trade organizations must also be involved.

Next Steps: Workshop participants also suggested that some national effort be made to collect data on, monitor, and analyze the volume of (1) non-U.S. computing professionals working offshore for U.S.-owned companies, (2) U.S. computing professionals working offshore for U.S.- and foreign-owned companies, and (3) U.S. computing professionals working domestically for foreign-owned companies.

BROADENING AND NURTURING
THE TALENT STREAM

Workshop participants expressed strong concerns about the growing difficulties in attracting talented individuals to computing professions, a difficulty reflected in declining undergraduate enrollments. This situation is exacerbated by the apparent difficulties in attracting and retaining people other than white males. Professionals in the industry reflect neither the demographics of today's population nor those expected in the future. Unless these conditions change, the field will diminish in vitality and even in size.

• **Greater and more effective efforts are needed to attract a more diverse group of people to computing professions to more closely reflect the demographic makeup of the country and assure survival of the field.** In particular, women and non-Asian minorities ought to be encouraged to choose and continue in professions in computing fields.

Next Steps: Given its dependence on a quality work force, industry has a stake in attracting good people. Trade associations (e.g., the Computer and Business Equipment Manufacturers Association (CBEMA), the Information Technology Association of America (ITAA), the Semiconductor Industry Association (SIA), the Electronic Industries Association (EIA), and the American Electronics Association (AEA)) are a logical vehicle for public outreach activities that focus on interesting applications and challenges. Professional organizations (e.g., the Association for Computing Machinery (ACM), the Institute for Electrical and Electronics Engineers (IEEE), the Computing Research Association (CRA), and the Institute of Scientific Information (ISI)), some of which have student chapters, are a natural vehicle for disseminating information about courses of study and career paths.

Workshop participants agreed that increasing the diversity of computing professionals calls for leadership, information sharing, creativity, and perhaps most of all, sustained effort. A first step would be to gain a better understanding, through social science research, of why participation by women and underrepresented minorities has been disproportionately low and why, in particular, participation by women appears to have been declining.

Participants noted that efforts aimed at attracting underrepresented groups should consist of specific activities that are appropriate in terms of gender, race, and ethnic background. Constraints on participation by women are not necessarily the same as those on participation by non-Asian minorities, and African Americans, Hispanics, and other minorities have different characteristics and needs. One minimum step discussed by several workshop participants was the establishment of a clearinghouse for ideas, programs, and experiences gained in efforts to attract and retain more women and non-Asian minorities in computing education and professional jobs.

PROVIDING FOR ONGOING TRAINING

The kinds of computing professional skills required by employers change relatively quickly, driving new and growing needs for training.

- **Changes in skill requirements will be a way of life for computing professionals.**

• **Frequent retraining may be necessary to meet shifting needs for skills.** The educational system can support this requirement both by producing graduates with broad and flexible skills and by contributing to more effective and more available retraining through interactions with industry.

• **Corporations must reconcile themselves to the financial and organizational commitments implied by continuous shifts in skill requirements.** Changes in skill requirements may result in some dislocation for individual employees. But rather than simply replacing employees, in the long run it may be more effective to update their technical skills while leveraging all of the other skills and capabilities required of employees to make organizations effective.

> *Next Steps:* Industry, professional organizations, and academia should recognize and support the trend toward lifelong learning. This concept is receiving increasing attention in other contexts (e.g., in various engineering disciplines). It is one that should become a part of the computing enterprise. While institutions—especially in industry—can provide resources to support retraining, individuals may require counseling and advice on how best to maintain their career currency.

ACTING ON IMPLICATIONS FOR EDUCATION

The large number and variety of apparently relevant education programs offered (computer science, computer engineering, information systems, information science, and management of information systems, among others) raises questions about the quality and appropriateness of available education.

• **Because skill needs are changing rapidly in industry, educational institutions need to produce graduates with the ability for and commitment to continuing lifelong learning.** In theory, these are consequences of good programs of basic education; in practice, it is not clear that these objectives are being met.

• **Although differences in educational curricula across institutions are consistent with the rich and dynamic nature of the field, an excessive degree of variation may be counterproductive.** For those who are interested in a computing career, the educational arena presents an array of choices so broad as to be confusing. Virtually every dimension, from labeling of programs to content, seems to vary, in every class of program. Perhaps improvements in taxonomies for data collection (see Chapter 2) can serve as a guide to educational institutions and students, helping to focus the skill development process.

• **While computing professional jobs are likely to continue to attract people from other fields, increasing skill requirements may call for more fundamental education in computer science and engineering than was needed in the past.** However, the trend toward greater cross-disciplinary interaction in addressing problems in computing and other domains might serve to fuel further in-migration. How different trends will balance out is unclear at this time.

> *Next Steps:* Workshop participants agreed that better definition of degree programs (categories and essential content) is needed and that fewer program categories would be desirable. Both would be of value to employers and prospective students. The CSTB and professional organizations could play a role in helping to better inform employers and prospective students about the various types of programs.

IMPROVING THE LINKAGE BETWEEN SCHOOL AND WORK

Another qualitative dimension of education is the fit between what is taught to students and the skills employers seek in filling their jobs. There will never be a perfect fit between the two, since educators focus on teaching students how to think and apply concepts, whereas most employers focus immediately on acquisition and application of specific, job-related skills (including skills in communication and collaboration). But workshop discussions suggested that there may be middle ground to explore; it may be possible to work within the framework of the traditional computer science and engineering educational programs to do more to develop skills relevant to the workplace. Also, as long as there continues to be a range of different programs, different types of schools and programs could concentrate on different types of skills and preparation.

> *Next Steps:* Options should be explored for greater interaction between industry and universities on matters of curriculum. Workshop participants recognized that this may be easier said than done. Given natural tendencies to insularity in both sectors, better mechanisms need to be established to facilitate communication. Some participants suggested that periodic workshops and/or conferences organized by organizations with solid connections and reputations in both academic and industrial communities could be effective vehicles for meeting this need.
> Exposure of students and, in particular, teachers to real-world problems and working conditions was encouraged by work-

shop participants from industry. Opportunities for students to work for a limited time in industry could be achieved through cooperative or work-study programs, summer jobs, or internships; summer or part-time opportunities could be provided to teachers.

IMPROVING DATA GATHERING AND ANALYSIS

The biggest obstacle to specific assessments of and recommendations for the computing professional labor market is the absence of adequate data on the existing skill base and job mix.

• **Available data are inadequate to guide employers, students, educators, and policymakers.** Both the kinds of data and delays in their publication pose problems. For example, data that are updated every 4 to 5 years will be inconsistent with technology and industry dynamics that change as quickly as those for computing. Because acquiring a comprehensive set of skills data could be prohibitively costly, modest insights might be obtained by collecting and analyzing skills assessments that, according to workshop participants, are currently being undertaken in industry and government.

• **A robust high-level taxonomy of computing professionals is needed.** Currently, data are collected using taxonomies or sets of job titles (see Box 2.1) that are too detailed and too prone to obsolescence as skills needed in real jobs change. For example, "hardware professionals," "software professionals," and "deployment professionals" (responsible for supporting and facilitating the effective use of systems; see Chapter 3) could be developed as gross categories of computing professionals that could have more lasting meaning than do the current large, but inappropriate, sets of occupational titles. However, a high-level taxonomy alone will not provide information on shifting skill requirements; meeting this need requires developing better, more detailed occupational data that take into account shifting technology and industry dynamics.

• **A major need is community agreement on how to label different types of computing professionals and whom to count in each category.** But workshop participants differed on how to implement these changes: academic participants placed a high premium on degree and skill attainment, and industrial and government participants focused more on the nature of the work to be done and the skills applied. This disparity in perspective is not surprising; it reflects the greater challenge evident in industry and government to adapt job descriptions to evolving technology and applications. Thus a number of nonacademic workshop participants referred to skills assessments they have conducted for their employees and clients and emphasized the evolution of job titles and progressions.

• **It is necessary to identify and evaluate changes in portfolios of skills associated with jobs, occupations, and individuals.** Like portfolios containing stocks and bonds, portfolios of skills are subject to change over time in their individual components and in the volume of each component. A job taxonomy is needed that partitions jobs into sets that are equivalent in terms of the skills required. A similar taxonomy for individuals is needed to partition workers into groups with sets of embodied skills that are equivalent. Finally, one must also be able to convert functions required on the job to skills possessed by workers before one can meaningfully assess the strength of the fit between workers and jobs. To properly gauge shifting skill requirements, it is necessary to build on a greater understanding of shifts in technology and industry dynamics.

• **The proposed high-level taxonomy should be related to portfolios of skills, providing a vehicle for tracking shifts in skill requirements that is independent of changing preferences in job titles.** For example, the high-level taxonomy category "software professionals" might include skills that range from simple programming tasks to sophisticated database design or other software development skills. Over time, some skills will diminish in importance as others become more important (see Chapter 3); it is important to track both the details of change and the gross numbers of computing professionals employed in hardware, software, and deployment.

> *Next Steps:* Workshop participants agreed that the Bureau of Labor Statistics and the National Science Foundation should develop more realistic taxonomies for data gathering. Those taxonomies should be based on a broader, more contemporary view of the field. Toward that end, these agencies should involve the computing professional community, drawing on professional organizations, trade associations, the National Research Council, and other vehicles for achieving broad-based, consensus input on more appropriate ways of describing the dynamic and rapidly changing market for computing professionals.

NOTE

1. Follow-up meetings have already begun and have included representatives of statistical agencies, professional organizations, and others, as well as CSTB and OSEP.

APPENDIXES

A

Comparison of Data Sources and Data

Betty M. Vetter
Commission on Professionals in Science and Technology

INTRODUCTION

As a relatively new field, computer science has not yet developed a classic set of definitions to describe what kinds of specialists to include in the field and what kinds to exclude when organizing information on human resources. Thus, in computer science and technology even more than in other fields of science and engineering with longer histories, one encounters variations in supposedly similar data derived from different sources.

Data Needed to Assess Supply and Demand

In general, two kinds of data are needed to assess supply and demand in any field: direct data such as number of degrees awarded, number of persons employed in the field, and particular demographic or other data about those persons; and indirect data, which are used to assess present demand and potential supply or demand. Indirect data include information on salaries, demographic changes, student plans and aspirations, and legislative changes such as those dealing with immigration or with particular appropriations, such as research budgets.

NOTE: A paper prepared for a computer science and technology workshop sponsored by the Computer Science and Telecommunications Board and the Office of Scientific and Engineering Personnel of the National Research Council, and held at the National Academy of Sciences Beckman Center, Irvine, California, October 28-29, 1991.

Sources of Direct Data

The sources of direct data on human resources in computer science and technology include the National Center for Education Statistics (NCES), which conducts an annual survey of earned degrees; the National Research Council (NRC), with its ongoing survey of new doctorates awarded and its biennial survey of the doctoral population; the Engineering Manpower Commission (EMC), which collects both enrollment and degree data in computer engineering and in computer technology; and the Computing Research Association (CRA), with its annual Taulbee survey of computer science departments. The Taulbee survey provides information on Ph.D.s awarded in computer science and computer engineering, data on doctoral enrollments in these fields, placement information for new Ph.D.s accepting academic positions, and faculty statistics in responding departments, including some estimates of future demand.

An additional source of direct data will be the 1991 report of the Conference Board of the Mathematical Sciences (CBMS), which surveys mathematics, statistics, and computer science departments every five years or so and reports on bachelor's degrees awarded. Data for the 1990-1991 school year, derived from that survey, have not yet been released, but this analysis includes some of the findings, used with permission.

Other sources of direct data on personnel employed in computer science and technology include the Bureau of Labor Statistics (BLS), which uses sample surveys to define various working populations; the Office of Personnel Management (OPM), which supplies data on federal employment in these fields; and the National Science Foundation (NSF), which sponsors or helps to sponsor surveys of Ph.D. recipients and their post-graduation plans, surveys of the experience of recent science and engineering graduates in the job market, and surveys of working scientists and engineers that aggregate information from several surveys. Information on subsections of the work force, specifically on faculty, is available from the BLS, the NSF, the NRC biennial survey of doctorates, the CRA, and the CBMS.

Sources of Indirect Data

Indirect data relating to current and potential scientists and engineers come from a number of sources.

• The Census Bureau, for example, provides data on the numbers of Americans who are born and die each year and on the occupations of a sample of Americans as reported for the decennial census. As of this writing, no occupational information is yet available from the 1990 census, but census data are used in projecting degree data for the future, based on the number of college-age students.

• The Cooperative Institutional Research Program, carried out at the University of California at Los Angeles, surveys a sample of all freshmen each year, asking, among other things, about their college plans. This survey provides useful information about potential bachelor's graduates four to six years later.

• The Institute for International Education's annual surveys of foreign students studying in the United States give some field information.

• The American Mathematical Society and the Mathematical Association of America surveys of Ph.D.s in mathematics offer a useful companion study to the Taulbee survey.

• The National Science Foundation is also an indirect source of data obtained in several studies that it supports but that are carried out by others, and it is the sole publisher of much of the data obtained by others under contract to the NSF, such as the NRC.

• Finally, salary information, which is an important indirect indicator of demand, is reported regularly by the College Placement Council, the American Association of University Professors (AAUP), and the College and University Personnel Association (CUPA) and can be compared with salaries reported in the Taulbee survey, and, most importantly, with those reported in other fields. The CUPA report distinguishes between public and private sector salaries and provides salary data by both rank and field. The AAUP survey does not report salaries by field, but instead groups institutions into categories, and reports salaries by rank within each category. This does not allow distinguishing the salaries of computer scientists from the salaries of faculty in other subject areas. One more salary report, by field, is conducted regularly by Oklahoma State University for institutions belonging to the National Association of State Universities and Land-Grant Colleges.

Additionally, the NRC biennial survey of the doctoral population in the United States provides salary information; employment, unemployment, and underemployment rates; and information on field of employment vs. field of Ph.D., which provides another indicator of the balance in supply and demand in a field. Unfortunately, the NRC no longer publishes these data, and the NSF publication procedures have become so slow that even in the last quarter of 1991, no published information was yet available on the 1989 survey.

Why the Data Differ

Some of these several surveys include the "same" information, such as degrees awarded, and might therefore be expected to provide some identical or at least highly similar statistics. Actually, this is almost never the case. Reasons for differences in data reported on similar populations include differences in taxonomy, such as definition of the field; differences in time frames covered by surveys (fiscal years, academic years, calendar years, and/or different starting and stopping places in the calendar); differences in the cutoff date for a survey, and importantly, differences in the person or persons responding to the survey—e.g., individuals reporting on themselves (as in the NRC Doctorate Records File), reporting by registrars (as in the NCES degree surveys), or reporting by deans or department heads (as in the EMC surveys). Differences also occur if Canada is included (as in the Taulbee surveys).

Further differences occur, even in what are purportedly 100 percent samples, because some individuals or institutions do not respond. Treatment of the non-respondents may include estimating from previous years, or omitting entirely.

None of these many surveys is necessarily either wrong or right, but understanding the differences is important in interpreting the data.

The differences found in the reporting of degrees awarded or other data based on 100 percent samples pale in comparison with the differences found in data reported from sample surveys of the numbers of persons employed in computer science and technology. Substantial differences continue to exist even when the survey population is limited to individuals with the doctorate.

The reasons for such discrepancies include all of those mentioned above, plus differences in sample population bases, sampling and weighing procedures, and response rates, and differences in the date that the survey "snapshot" is made. There may also be significant differences in data that have been aggregated because of small sample sizes.

Despite obvious differences in data on similar populations, however, data from one source may be used to enhance and illuminate data from another. When the differences are very large, as is the case for some of the data examined in this paper, it is usually worthwhile to try to find out why.

COMPARING AVAILABLE DATA ON SUPPLY

The easiest and potentially the most compatible data on the supply of computer scientists and computer engineers should be degrees awarded, since all of the various sources for degree data attempt to use 100 percent samples.

Bachelor's Degrees

At the bachelor's degree level, reports of degrees awarded in computer science in 1989 vary from 8,796 reported by CRA (and apparently including Canadian departments but limited to U.S. institutions awarding Ph.D.s) to 30,963 reported by NCES, which includes only the United States (Table A.1). For 1990, there are again two data sources, but not the same ones; CRA reported 9,037 degrees awarded compared with 21,704 reported by CBMS. Is the difference accounted for by departmental coverage, definitional differences, or both, or perhaps something else? The CBMS data include computer science degrees awarded both by departments of mathematics and by departments of computer science, including some joint mathematics-computer science degrees.

Data on the number of bachelor's degrees awarded in computer engineering should be easier to compare, since there is one addi-

TABLE A.1 B.S. Computer Science and Computer Engineering Degrees Reported, 1986 to 1991

Year	CRA	NCES	EMC	CBMS
Computer Science				
1985				
1986	10,947	42,195		32,348
1987	10,540	39,927		
1988	10,759	34,896		
1989	8,796	30,963		
1990	9,037			21,704
1991	8,232			
Computer Engineering				
1986		2,192	4,999	
1987	2,103	2,021	5,012	
1988	1,928	2,115	4,275	
1989	1,810	2,198	4,398	
1990	1,628		4,355	
1991	1,632			

NOTE: Data from annual and other surveys of the Computing Research Association (CRA), National Center for Education Statistics (NCES), Engineering Manpower Commission (EMC), and Conference Board of the Mathematical Sciences (CBMS).

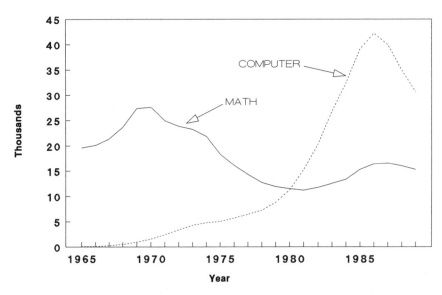

FIGURE A.1 Bachelor's degrees awarded in mathematics and computer science, 1965 to 1989. SOURCE: National Center for Education Statistics (1965-1989) and unpublished data from the National Science Foundation.

tional source of data, and there are many fewer engineering schools than there are degree-granting colleges and universities. But the number of graduates reported for 1989 varies from 1,810 reported by CRA (which apparently includes no Canadian graduates and is limited to degrees awarded only in those U.S. schools that also award doctorates in computer engineering), to 2,115 reported by NCES, to 4,398 reported by EMC. Why is the number reported by the EMC twice as high as the others? The reason for the large differences is not apparent.

Obviously, students who might have been attracted to mathematics might also have been attracted to computer science. Indeed, as the number of computer science degrees increased during the 1970s, the number of mathematics degrees dropped steadily (Figure A.1). Some of the degrees counted by one data source as computer science degrees may be counted as mathematics degrees in other data sets. The CBMS data for 1989-1990 indicate that 16 percent of the computer science bachelor's degrees were awarded in departments of mathematics, and the remaining 84 percent were awarded by computer science departments. Since the NCES data usually are reported by registrars and the CBMS data by department chairs, it is possible that some of the degrees that might be assigned to mathematics by the department head could be assumed by the registrar to be computer science, or vice versa.

It is noteworthy that both mathematics and computer science bachelor's degrees are now declining.

Master's Degrees

At the master's degree level there are no comparative databases, so that degree data from NCES are assumed to be correct. It is apparent, however, based on discrepancies seen at the bachelor's level, that such an assumption is, at best, questionable.

Doctoral Degrees

Data on doctoral degrees awarded should be fully compatible, since the number of schools awarding doctorates is limited and all of them should be included in each of the available data sources. Further, after a dozen years of reporting on these degrees, it should be possible to assume some agreement about what constitutes a Ph.D. degree in computer science or in computer engineering.

Compared with the data on bachelor's degrees awarded, the data on doctoral degrees are in considerably closer agreement. However, they still fail to match within a few percentage points.

Number of Ph.D.s Awarded

In 1989, the most recent year for which all databases have reported, computer science doctorates numbered 538 (NCES), 612 (NRC), or 625 (CRA) (Table A.2). For computer engineering that year, the four data sources report 74 (NCES), 117 (NRC), 182 (CRA), or 277 (EMC) doctoral degrees awarded. The top-to-bottom difference is 274 percent! Without knowing for sure, I must assume that this immense difference lies in how these various sources define computer engineering.

Combining the computer science and computer engineering Ph.D.s narrows the gaps a little and indicates that some of the doctorates reported as computer science degrees in some data sets may be reported as computer engineering degrees in others. Since no computer science data are available from EMC, we must omit its computer engineering data for this comparison. The combined figure for Ph.D.s awarded in computer science and computer engineering in 1989 is 612 (NCES), 729 (NRC), or 807 (CRA)—still an uncomfortable 32 percent difference from top to bottom (Table A.3). Are 195 of these

TABLE A.2 Ph.D. Computer Science and Computer Engineering
Degrees Reported, 1986 to 1990

Year	CRA	NCES	NRC	EMC
Computer Science				
1986	412	344	399	
1987	466	374	450	
1988	577	428	514	
1989	625	538	612	
1990	734		704	
Computer Engineering				
1986		56	77	176
1987	93	57	61	205
1988	167	77	92	262
1989	182	74	117	277
1990	173		132	399

NOTE: Data from annual and other surveys of the Computing Research Association
(CRA), National Center for Education Statistics (NCES), National Research Council
(NRC), and Engineering Manpower Commission (EMC).

graduates from Canadian institutions? The Taulbee report for 1990
indicates only 25 Canadian Ph.D.s in computer science, and none in
computer engineering. The data sets that report 1990 doctorate awards
at this time agree fairly well in computer science, but are far apart for
computer engineering.

The early increase in bachelor's-level computer science degrees
came at the expense of mathematics degrees, and that appears to
have happened also for doctoral degrees through the first half of the
1970s (Figure A.2). Then as computer science degrees leveled off for
a decade, so also did degrees in mathematics, through 1985. Both
fields have seen increases in each year since 1985 in the number of
doctorates awarded, and at least a part of this increase appears to be
made up of American citizens.

*Demographic Characteristics of Computer Science and Computer
Engineering Ph.D.s*

Regardless of the source of data, it is apparent that foreign citizens come a close second to white, American males in dominating
the Ph.D. recipients in both computer science and computer engineering (Table A.4). But once again, the data sources do not agree on
the extent of dominance by foreign graduates.

TABLE A.3 Combined Computer Science and Computer
Engineering Ph.D. Degrees Reported, 1986 to 1990

Year	CRA	NCES	NRC
1986		400	476
1987	559	431	511
1988	744	505	606
1989	807	612	729
1990	907		836

NOTE: Data from annual and other surveys of the Computing Research
Association (CRA), National Center for Education Statistics (NCES), and
National Research Council (NRC).

In each of the three sources that provide information about the
citizenship of doctoral graduates, the data refer to foreign graduates
on temporary visas rather than the more inclusive "non-U.S. citizens." Unfortunately, the three data sources for computer science
(CRA, NRC, and NCES) are not exactly the same as the three for
computer engineering (CRA, NRC, and EMC). Further, we cannot
get exactly the same information from all data sources for either 1989
or 1990.

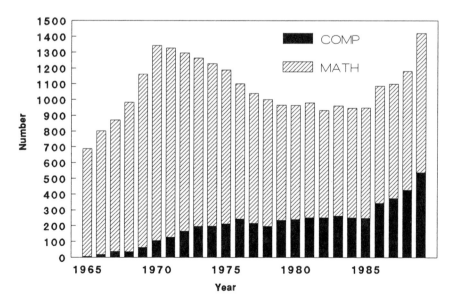

FIGURE A.2 Ph.D. degrees awarded in mathematics and computer science,
1965 to 1989. SOURCE: National Center for Education Statistics (1965-1989).

TABLE A.4   Individuals Receiving Ph.D.s in 1989 in Computer
Science and Computer Engineering

Data Source (Year)	Number (Percent of Total)					
	Total	Foreign	Women	Asians	Hispanics	African Americans
Computer Science						
CRA (90)	734	331 (45.1)	97 (13.2)	212 (28.9)	8 (1.1)	3 (0.4)
NRC (89)	612	179 (29.2)	107 (17.5)	52 (8.5)	4 (0.7)	1 (0.2)
NCES (89)	538	205 (38.1)	81 (15.1)	42 (7.8)	4 (0.7)	2 (0.4)
Computer Engineering						
CRA (90)	173	62 (35.8)	17 (9.8)	69 (39.9)	3 (1.7)	1 (0.6)
NRC (89)	117	65 (55.6)	12 (10.3)	8 (6.8)	1 (0.9)	0 (0.0)
EMC (89)	277	108 (39.0)	33 (11.9)	11 (4.7)	1 (0.4)	3 (1.1)

NOTE: Data from annual and other surveys of the Computing Research Association
(CRA), National Research Council (NRC), National Center for Education Statistics (NCES),
and Engineering Manpower Commission (EMC).

The NRC reports that 178 foreign students on temporary visas
received a doctorate in computer science in 1989 (29.1 percent of total
awards) and that in computer engineering, 65 of the 117 new graduates (55.6 percent) had temporary visas (Table A.5). NCES data show
that 205 graduates with temporary visas were among the 538 Ph.D.
recipients in computer science (38.1 percent) but do not provide data
by citizenship for recipients of computer engineering doctorates. EMC
data indicate that 108 of the 277 Ph.D. degrees awarded in computer
engineering (39 percent) were earned by foreign students on temporary visas. The CRA figures for 1989 show that 248 of the 625 computer science graduates in 1989 (39.7 percent) were foreign and 62 of
the 173 computer engineering graduates in 1990 (35.8 percent) were
foreign.

It is easy to see how the Taulbee survey (CRA) data for foreign
citizens might be higher than the other data sets in computer science,
because Canadian graduates are included. But only 25 Canadian
recipients are included in the 1990 figures (3.4 percent of the total) so
that this does not explain the large discrepancy. Even reducing the
numbers to percentages shows that the foreign percentage in computer science differs by 15 percentage points, and in computer engineering by 20 percentage points.

There is general agreement about the percentage of women in
both computer science and computer engineering, and the general

TABLE A.5 Citizenship and Visa Status of Computer Scientists and Computer Engineers Receiving Ph.D.s, 1980 to 1990

	Computer Scientists					Computer Engineers			
Year	Total	U.S.	Perm. Visa	Temp. Visa	Cit. Un-known	Total	U.S. & Perm. Visa	Temp. Visa	Cit. Un-known
1980	218	156	13	43	6	62	37	25	0
1981	232	168	20	40	4	71	46	24	1
1982	220	143	12	59	6	72	46	24	1
1983	286	180	27	72	7	83	45	36	2
1984	295	178	17	89	11	56	33	21	2
1985	310	189	24	89	8	55	24	25	5
1986	399	202	47	123	27	77	37	37	3
1987	450	243	32	143	32	62	29	32	1
1988	515	284	42	176	13	100	38	57	5
1989	612	338	58	178	38	117	45	65	7
1990	704	343	53	263	45	132	46	86	0

NOTE: Data from annual and other surveys of the National Research Council's (NRC) Office of Scientific and Engineering Personnel.

absence of Hispanic and African American doctorate holders is noted in all data sets. However, the percentage of Asian graduates is much higher in the CRA data than in either of the other two data sets. The reason for the discrepancy is not obvious.

Looking at the citizenship status of computer scientists and engineers in the same data set (NRC) over time shows a rising number of both U.S. and foreign citizens over the past decade.

Although there are discrepancies in the data, all the data sources show three general trends:

• a very high and growing proportion of foreign students among Ph.D. graduates, and thus among graduate students and teaching assistants;

• a very low proportion of women, and of African Americans and Hispanics of either sex; and

• a high representation of Asian Americans, relative to their representation in the population. However, relative to all Asian doctorate recipients, Asian Americans represent only about one tenth of the total.

DATA ON THE CURRENT LABOR FORCE

Numerical differences in gross data on the U.S. work force as reported by two major sources would be expected to differ substan-

TABLE A.6 Mathematicians and Computer Scientists in the U.S. Work Force, 1990 and 1988

Data Source (Year)	Math	CS	Subtotal	Faculty Math	CS	Total
BLS (90)			805,000	54,000	22,000	881,000
NSF (88)	168,600	708,300	876,900			876,900

NOTE: Data from Bureau of Labor Statistics (BLS, 1990) and National Science Foundation (NSF, 1988).

tially. Surprisingly, they yield the best match found to date between two or more data sets among the data sets reviewed so far in this paper.

The Bureau of Labor Statistics reports a total of 805,000 mathematicians and computer scientists as of January 1990, plus 22,000 higher-education teachers of computer science and 54,000 mathematics faculty members, for a total U.S. math and computer science work force of 881,000 (Table A.6). The National Science Foundation estimates a work force of 708,300 computer specialists and 168,600 mathematical scientists for 1988 (the most recent data available from NSF) for a total math and computer science work force of 876,900. Obviously by coincidence, the total numbers differ by less than 1 percent.

However, examination of just one segment of the work force—college and university employees—shows much larger differences reported among available data sets. Further, data available from one database are not available from another, so that, for example, tenured or tenure-track faculty cannot always be distinguished from non-tenure-track faculty or other employees in the numbers given. Some data sets include data only for Ph.D.s, while others give total faculty or total academic employment without reference to highest degree earned. Thus, no matter how much we try, it is easy to mix apples and oranges.

It is particularly difficult to sort out data on faculty from data describing other academic employees; to determine what proportion of each group is made up of women; and, among the faculty, to determine how many are tenured. Table A.7, which includes data on computer specialists employed in academic institutions, indicates that, for the two data sets that break out the computer scientists from the computer engineers, the data on computer engineers are a closer match than the data on computer scientists. The NRC reports almost twice as many computer scientists employed in academic institutions as

TABLE A.7 Ph.D. Computer/Information Specialists in Academic Institutions by Tenure Status

	CBMS	BLS	NRC			CRA		
			Total	Comp./Info. Spec.	Sys. Design Eng.	Total	Comp. Sci.	Comp. Eng.
Total	4,189	22,000	7,686	6,553	1,113	4,525	3,567	958
Women	670	6,000	739	707	32	243		
Tenured	2,810		3,415	2,759	656	3,501	2,782	719
Women			212	205	7	243	213	30
Asst. prof.						1,210	979	231
Women						113	96	17
Assoc. prof.						978	774	204
Women						89	80	9
Full prof.						1,313	940	373
Women						41	37	4
In tenure track			1,783	1,636	147			
Women			194	180	14			
Not in tenure track			633	623	10	486	405	81
Women			38	35	3			
Tenure not applicable			882	762	120	364	293	71
Women			151	149	2			
No report			973	773	200			
Women			144	138	6			
Non-teach. resch. faculty						174	145	29
Postdocs						116	85	31
Other faculty (e.g., visitors)						248	208	40

NOTE: The NRC data are from the 1989 Survey of Doctorate Recipients, the CRA data are from the 1989-1990 Taulbee survey, the CBMS data are from the survey of the same year, and the BLS estimates are as of January 1, 1990. The BLS estimates also include non-doctoral faculty, but neither number nor percentage breakouts are available.

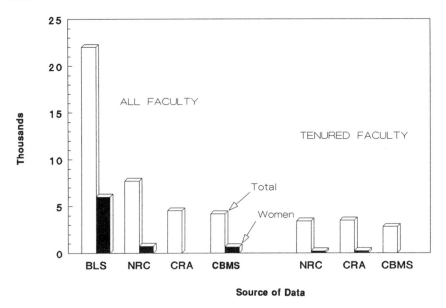

FIGURE A.3   Ph.D. computer specialists employed in academic institutions and those with tenure.   SOURCES: Data from National Research Council (1990), Computing Research Association (1990), Conference Board of the Mathematical Sciences (1991), and estimates from the Bureau of Labor Statistics.

does the CRA. Combining the data on computer scientists and computer engineers from both sources (NRC and CRA) and comparing it with the CBMS total shows closer correlation, but still with a significant difference (Figure A.3).

Although the BLS data are reported, the figures are not comparable with those from the other data sources, which are limited to Ph.D.s. Nonetheless, the BLS reports 22,000 computer science faculty in 1989, whereas NSF, reporting on NRC data from the biennial survey of the doctoral work force, notes only 6,553 academically employed Ph.D.s in computer science in 1989. Could this mean that 70 percent of higher-education faculty in computer science do not have a doctorate? Almost surely, it does not mean that.

The Taulbee survey for the 1990-1991 academic year records 3,567 individuals employed in 135 of 136 computer science departments, including 2,724 tenure-track faculty. The best comparison, from the NRC survey of 1989, is 4,395 tenured or tenure-track faculty, in a total of 6,553 academically employed Ph.D.s.

DEMOGRAPHIC CHARACTERISTICS OF THE
CURRENT LABOR FORCE

Significant differences are found also in the sketchy data available on the demographics of the U.S. computer science and engineering work force.

The BLS reports that in 1990 32.5 percent of computer scientists and systems analysts were women, 5.6 percent were African American, and 3 percent were Hispanic. The NSF, which has no data past 1986, has estimated that in 1988, 31 percent of employed computer specialists were women, 0.4 percent were African American, 1.2 percent were Hispanic, and 6.6 percent were Asian.

The CRA does not attempt to examine anything but the doctoral population, and that only in academe. NRC data show the doctoral population in 1989 to include 11.6 percent women, 1 percent African Americans, 1.8 percent Hispanics, 0.2 percent Native Americans, and 12.2 percent Asians. Certainly there is general agreement that none of these groups except Asians is adequately represented in computer science or computer engineering. The level of under-representation for African American and Hispanic participants is quite different in the BLS and NSF data sets on the labor force.

A few other demographic facts are not in dispute. One is that computer science Ph.D.s are younger than their fellows in mathematics or in the physical sciences (Figure A.4). This does not mean that computer science is necessarily less likely than the other science and engineering fields to experience shortages of qualified faculty after the student-age population increases again in the latter half of the 1990s. But it does mean that faculty replacements will not necessarily be required in large numbers at the same time that growth in the student body exerts pressure for more faculty members.

The bottom line is that we do not know for sure how many individuals of what citizenship, what sex, and what race or ethnicity earn degrees at any level in computer science or computer engineering. We do not know for sure how many people are working in the broad area of computer science and technology, or how many are seeking employment requiring such expertise. We do not know whether there are significant numbers of persons with appropriate training to step in and fill available jobs if jobs should suddenly open up, or whether such jobs could be filled only with persons having lower qualifications than those being sought. In other words, we do not know whether supply and demand are now in balance for this broad area of expertise.

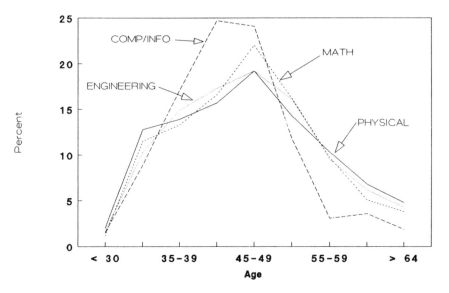

FIGURE A.4   Ages of employed computer science Ph.D.s compared to ages of employed Ph.D. holders in engineering, mathematics, and physical sciences, 1989. SOURCE: National Science Foundation (1990).

THE FUTURE

Data Indicators of Demand

All of us are concerned with whether supply will match, over-match, or undermatch demand in the computer sciences for baccalaureate-level and for Ph.D. specialists. For dealing with the future, of course, no data exist. We operate with indicators of probable oversupply or undersupply, including unemployment rates and rates for starting salaries compared with those for other fields (and changes in starting salaries, where increases substantially above those offered in other fields are a definite indicator of a current shortage of graduates to fill open positions). Federal budgets, and changes in those budgets that affect research opportunities, also are considered, insofar as they are known.

Another indicator of trends in supply and demand is the amount of classified advertising and display advertising for the various specialties of the computer sciences. Whether the number of column inches of advertising space in the "Help Wanted" columns is rising or falling over time helps to identify the trends of undersupply or oversupply. Unfortunately, there is no regular index of change in the amount of advertising for positions for computer scientists. Previously, the Demand Index for Scientists and Engineers, provided by the New York firm of Deutsch, Shea and Evans, counted column inches of advertising (classified and display) in a combination of several large daily papers and in several professional science and engineering journals, producing a 3-month average rolling index of such advertising as it related to the "norm" starting date of 1961. Unfortunately, that index ceased to be compiled after 1989—a real setback to efforts to keep track of relative changes in advertising for the science and engineering professions as a whole, and a particular loss during the past 24 months when the nation has been experiencing its strongest recession in a decade or more.

What We Do Not Know—and What We Need to Know—About Current Supply and Demand

There is no current, dependable measure to tell us, at any one time, whether supply and demand are in or out of balance, and by how much. Examining some of what we know (or what I thought we knew when I began this exercise) and listing some of what we do not know lead to the conclusion that it is also important to be sure that what we think we know actually is known. Although this appears obvious, I confess that I know less about the data on supply *or* demand in the computer sciences than I thought I knew a few weeks before I started diving, far too confidently, into this assignment.

I thought I knew, within a very few percentage points, how many computer scientists and engineers are graduating each year at each degree level; approximately how many faculty are currently employed teaching computer science; and within wide margins, about how many people now make their living in the United States based on their knowledge and use of computers. While an exact number for each of these questions is not required, it is vital to understand why multiple data sets provide different numbers, particularly when wide differences occur.

• We need to know for sure how many graduates are produced, and we need to know what skills and knowledge can be assumed to have been acquired by persons earning degrees at different levels in computer science or engineering. The taxonomy needs to be clarified, so that as nearly as possible, we all mean the same thing when using the same words to describe specialists in computer science and technology.

• We need to know at least a bit better than we do now how many people currently are working in computer science, and particularly, how many of them are in industry, in academic institutions, and in government. We need to know something about the distribution of levels of skills within this work force and whether a different mix of levels of skills might result in better utilization of talent and training.

• We need to know in considerably more detail about our academic work force for computer science, including whether currently funded faculty positions are filled; how many such positions exist; whether vacant positions (if any) are for teaching slots, for research, for administration, or for some combinations of these tasks; and what the incumbents in occupied positions are responsible for doing. We also need to know the demographic characteristics of incumbents, and of the applicant pool.

Forecasting the Future

We have seen some of the difficulties in analyzing the current balance in supply and demand for computer specialists. Even more difficult, of course, is projecting the future, with its many unknown characteristics, of which the most important undoubtedly is the state of the economy. Lacking this information, we must apply whatever information is available to provide the best possible estimates of future needs and the likelihood of their being fulfilled.

We need to recognize the difference, in examining future scenarios, between "need" and "demand." My own definition is that "demand" is "need plus money." No position can be filled until funding is available to pay the salary, no matter how much an individual may be needed to carry out necessary tasks.

Intuitively, we sense that the need for persons with a wide knowledge of how to design, to build, to assemble, to program, and to utilize computers will continue to grow, probably at a faster pace than Americans are prepared to practice those skills by virtue of their education and training.

As the number of college-age Americans starts to rise again beginning in 1995, the numbers of faculty needed both for growth and replacement also will rise. While funds for doctoral research in the area of computers, or in other areas that require use of computers, may continue to be below the amounts that American researchers need, or think they need, perhaps more of those researchers may find teaching jobs in higher education, both to prepare students who major in these fields and to provide user skills to all college students.

There will be too few white, non-Hispanic males interested in these fields to fill our needs. Recruitment of women and of American minorities is essential. The alternative is to continue training and employing foreign graduates until they so dominate the field that almost no Americans will choose to enter it. This alternative also assumes that sufficient numbers of highly motivated, very bright young people from other countries will want to come to the United States to learn all they can, and then will want to stay here instead of returning home. It further assumes that immigration laws will continue to permit, and possibly to encourage, such immigration.

Throughout the next two decades, there will be periods of a temporary surplus of candidates relative to jobs for almost every occupation. Those who persist and who hone their skills and credentials will flourish despite these ups and downs. It also appears fairly certain that during the next two decades, there will be one or more periods involving a shortage of well-qualified candidates relative to available jobs for computer science occupations as well as for those in many related professional fields. What is not so certain is whether there will be a sufficiently large pool of capable, interested, and qualified persons coming out of high school from which to recruit computer or other related specialists. While the numbers of high school students will be sufficient, too few of them currently show the necessary levels of achievement in required background areas that would make them good candidates for recruitment. Whether that will change sufficiently and soon enough to protect the American investment in computer expertise, or whether our dependence on foreign students, foreign graduates, and even foreign workers will increase, is not yet clear.

The safest prophecies for the future, however, carefully omit both "data" and dates. I cannot tell how many computer specialists will be needed by what time; how many are likely to be needed at any particular period, at what level of training; or whether surpluses or shortages will occur in specific years. The most important question may be whether America can cope with imbalances, when they occur, in ways that will benefit the nation, or whether we will continue to lose ground to other nations.

BIBLIOGRAPHY

Astin, Alexander, et al. 1978-1991. *The American Freshman, Fall 1990*. Annual Series 1978-1990. Los Angeles: Cooperative Institutional Research Program of the American Council on Education and University of California, Los Angeles.

Bureau of Labor Statistics. 1990. *Employment and Earnings*. Washington, D.C.: Department of Labor, January.

Bush, George, and U.S. Governors. 1989. *Joint Statement from the President's Education Summit with Governors*, University of Virginia, Charlottesville, Va., September 27-28.

College Placement Council. 1991. *Salary Survey, Final Report 1991*. College Placement Council, Bethlehem, Pa., July.

Computing Research Association. 1990. *The 1988-1989 Taulbee Survey Report: The Computing Research Association's Survey on the Production and Employment of Ph.D.'s and Faculty in Computer Science and Engineering*. Washington, D.C.: Computing Research Association.

Computing Research Association. 1992. *The 1990-1991 Taulbee Survey Report: The Computing Research Association's Survey on the Production and Employment of Ph.D.'s and Faculty in Computer Science and Engineering*. Washington, D.C.: Computing Research Association.

Conference Board of the Mathematical Sciences. 1991. *Report on Survey of Departments in Mathematics, Statistics and Computer Science*. Draft tables and charts.

Dossey, John A., Ina V.S. Mullis, Mary M. Lindquist, and Donald Chambers. 1988. *The Mathematics Report Card: Trends and Achievement Based on the 1986 National Assessment*. Princeton, N.J.: Educational Testing Service.

Engineering Manpower Commission. 1991a. *Engineering and Technology Degrees, 1990*. Annual Series, 1972-1990. Washington, D.C.: American Association of Engineering Societies.

Engineering Manpower Commission. 1991b. *Engineering and Technology Enrollments, Fall 1990*. Annual Series, 1972-1990. Washington, D.C.: American Association of Engineering Societies.

Federal Coordinating Council for Science, Engineering and Technology. 1991. *First in the World by the Year 2000*. FCCSET Committee on Education and Human Resources. Washington D.C.: Office of Science and Technology Policy.

Gittelsohn, John E. 1989. "Surging Economy Spurs Many Asians to Return Home." *Chronicle of Higher Education*, Vol. A 11-12 (November 15).

Gries, David, and Dorothy Marsh. 1991. *The 1989-1990 Taulbee Survey Report*. Annual Series. Washington, D.C.: Computing Research Association.

Gries, David, and Dorothy Marsh. 1991. "CS Produced 734 Ph.D.s in 1989-90; CE Added 173 for a Total of 907." *Communications of the ACM* 34(January):6-10.

Higher Education Surveys. 1990. *Survey of Mathematics and Statistics Departments at Higher Education Institutions, Survey No. 5*. National Science Foundation, National Endowment for the Humanities, and the U.S. Department of Education. Washington, D.C.: National Science Foundation, December.

Huckenthohler, G.J. 1990. *Selected Data on Graduate Science/Engineering Students and Postdoctorates, Fall 1990*. NSF 90-324. Unpublished early release statistics, National Science Foundation, Washington, D.C.

Lapointe, Archie E., Nancy A. Mead, and Gary W. Phillips. 1989. *A World of Differences: An International Assessment of Mathematics and Science*. Princeton, N.J.: Educational Testing Service.

Long, Janice. 1990. "Changes in Immigration Law Eyed to Avert Shortage of U.S. Scientists." *Chemical and Engineering News*, August 20, pp. 19-20.

Madison, Bernard L., and Therese A. Hart. 1990. *A Challenge of Numbers: People in the Mathematical Sciences*. Committee on the Mathematical Sciences in the Year 2000, National Research Council. Washington, D.C.: National Academy Press.

Mathematical Sciences Education Board. 1991. *Moving Beyond Myths: Revitalizing Undergraduate Mathematics*. Committee on the Mathematical Sciences in the Year 2000, National Research Council. Washington, D.C.: National Academy Press.

Mullis, Ina V.S., John A. Dossey, Eugene H. Owen, and Gary W. Phillips. 1991. *The State of Mathematics Achievement.* Report No. 21-ST-03. Educational Testing Service, for the National Center for Education Statistics. Washington, D.C.: U.S. Government Printing Office, June.

National Center for Education Statistics. 1950-1989. *Earned Degrees Conferred by U.S. Colleges and Universities.* Annual Series, 1950-1984. Data for 1985 through 1989 unpublished.

National Research Council. 1991. *Summary Report 1990: Doctorate Recipients from United States Universities.* Series, 1972-1990. Washington D.C.: National Academy Press.

National Science Board. 1989. *Report of the NSB Committee on Foreign Involvement in U.S. Universities.* Washington, D.C.: U.S. Government Printing Office.

National Science Foundation. 1987. *U.S. Scientists and Engineers: 1986.* NSF 87-322, detailed statistical tables. Washington, D.C.: U.S. Government Printing Office.

National Science Foundation. 1988. *Characteristics of Doctoral Scientists and Engineers in the United States: 1987.* NSF 88-331. Washington, D.C.: U.S. Government Printing Office.

National Science Foundation. 1990. *Future Scarcities of Scientists and Engineers: Problems and Solutions.* Unpublished working draft, STIA Division of Policy Research and Analysis, Summer 1990, Washington, D.C.

National Science Foundation. 1991. *Early Release of Summary Statistics on Science and Engineering Doctorates, 1990.* Unpublished manuscript, STIA Division of Policy Research and Analysis, May, Washington, D.C.

National Science Foundation. 1991. *Natural Science and Engineering Degree Production in the 1990s.* Unpublished draft, STIA Division of Policy Research and Analysis, undated, Washington, D.C.

Office of Technology Assessment. 1991. *Federally Funded Research: Decisions for a Decade.* Washington D.C.: U.S. Government Printing Office, May.

Palca, Joseph. 1990. "Young Investigators at Risk." *Science* (July 27):351-353.

Silvestri, George, and John Lukaseiwicz. 1989. "Projections of Occupational Employment, 1988-2000." *Monthly Labor Review* 112 (November):42-64.

Task Force on Women, Minorities, and the Handicapped in Science and Technology. 1988 and 1989. *Changing America: The New Face of Science and Engineering.* Interim report, 1988, and final report, 1989. Washington, D.C.: U.S. Government Printing Office.

U.S. Department of Education. 1990. *Earned Degrees Conferred by Institutions of Higher Education.* Unpublished tables. Continuing series of annual publications since 1948.

Vetter, Betty M. (ed.). 1991. *Professional Women and Minorities: A Manpower Data Resource Service.* Ninth edition. Washington, D.C.: Commission on Professionals in Science and Technology, March.

White, John R. 1990. "President's Letter." *Communications of the ACM* 33 (No. 9, September):19-20.

B

U.S. Degree Programs in Computing

A. Joseph Turner
Department of Computer Science
Clemson University

INTRODUCTION

Many different titles are used for academic programs in computing in the United States. However, graduates of programs with such different titles as Computer Science, Information Systems, Information Science, Management Information Systems, Management of Information Systems, and Computer Engineering can be classified in various reports as having the same occupational specialty (such as computer specialist). This is undesirable because different types of programs produce graduates with quite different capabilities, and these different capabilities are not readily interchangeable as desirable preparation for different jobs.

Finding a solution to this problem is complicated by the fact that degree titles are not used in a consistent manner. Different titles are sometimes used to designate programs that are essentially the same, and the same title is sometimes used for programs that are quite different.

This paper provides an overview of programs in computing that are currently offered in the United States. The term *computing* as

---

NOTE: A paper prepared for a computer science and technology workshop sponsored by the Computer Science and Telecommunications Board and the Office of Scientific and Engineering Personnel of the National Research Council, and held at the National Academy of Sciences Beckman Center, Irvine, California, October 28-29, 1991.

used here refers generally to disciplines that emphasize fundamental concepts of computer software and hardware, or the development of software for applications in general domains such as business and management. Programs that emphasize computer hardware are only of peripheral interest here, as are programs that are oriented toward teaching skills or applications of computers, and programs that are oriented toward the management of computing resources. The primary interest is baccalaureate programs, but two-year and graduate programs are considered as well.

An overview of all programs is given in the next section, followed by a more detailed look at baccalaureate programs. Subsequent sections provide some comparison and characterization of baccalaureate programs, briefly discuss two-year and graduate programs, and offer some observations on the need for standardization and the need for further work to provide data and characterizations.

OVERVIEW OF PROGRAMS

As might be expected, several different degree designations (A.A., B.S., B.A., M.S., Ph.D., and others) are used for each of the various major programs (computer science, information systems, and so on). These programs have many different orientations, both in terms of the application domains that are addressed and the program objectives. The graduates of these different programs are not generally interchangeable in terms of their preparation for employment, and so distinctions in names (titles) are both appropriate and needed.

Two-Year Programs

At least 600 of the 2,340 two-year colleges in the United States offer at least one degree or certificate program in computing [2]. The degree programs are generally designated A.A., A.S., or A.A.S. Some of the program titles and the number of such programs (according to the *Chronicle Two-Year College Databook* [2]) include Computer and Information Science, 510; Computer Programming, 315; Data Processing, 240; Information Sciences and Systems, 120; Microprocessor Applications, 115; Computer Service Technician, 90; and CAD/CAM, 80.

Some general characteristics of these programs are the following:

• They are oriented toward skills acquisition and current technology;
• They are oriented toward the job market, usually with a strong local influence;

• They are intended to produce graduates for entry-level jobs; and

• They attract some students with a baccalaureate degree who want to change careers.

There is substantial variation among two-year programs with similar titles. For example, one program designated "Computer Science" can have a computing component that is similar to the computing component of some respectable four-year programs, while the computing component of another program with the same title can consist mostly of courses in various programming languages. Similarly, "Microprocessor Applications" can emphasize programming in Basic, or its "computing" component can consist mostly of courses in word processing, spreadsheets, and database software use.

Curriculum recommendations for two-year programs were provided by the Association for Computing Machinery (ACM) in the late 1970s, but these recommendations are now outdated. The ACM Two-Year College Education Committee currently has an effort under way to produce new recommendations for two-year programs. This committee has grouped these programs into four areas: (1) computing and engineering technology (hardware oriented), (2) computing in information processing (information systems oriented), (3) computing science (computer science oriented), and (4) computer support services (e.g., operations). (The committee has also listed a fifth area, computing for other disciplines, but it is not relevant here.)

Baccalaureate Programs

As is the case for two-year programs, baccalaureate programs in computing have many different titles. Most existing programs have a major designation similar to one of the following:

• Computer Engineering
• Computer Science and Engineering
• Computer Science
• Computer Information Systems
• Information Science
• Information Systems
• Management Information Systems
• Management of Information Systems

Most of the degrees are designated B.S., but there are also B.A. degrees and variations such as B.C.S. (Bachelor of Computer Science). A difference in degree designation is not necessarily meaningful, however.

For example, a designation of B.A. is generally thought to denote a program that provides a broad, general education with a less intensive major than might be expected in a B.S. program. However, some institutions offer both B.A. and B.S. programs with identical requirements, and each graduate can choose the designation that is used on the diploma.

Except for some B.A. programs, most of these programs are intended to prepare graduates for entry into the computing profession. They ideally emphasize foundations and principles, rather than skills and current technology, with the goal of preparing graduates for lifelong learning, career growth, and further study. These programs are discussed further in "Baccalaureate Programs" below.

Master's Programs

Master's-level programs generally can be classified as (1) traditional (or research oriented), with degree designations such as M.S., or (2) professional, with degree designations such as M.C.S. (Master of Computer Science) or M.B.A. The degree designation is not a reliable indicator of the nature of a master's-level program, however. For example, many, if not most, M.S. programs in computer science have a non-thesis option, and many of these also have a course-work-only option.

Master's degrees are offered in the areas listed above for baccalaureate degrees. Accurate information on the number of master's-level programs does not appear to be available. However, *Peterson's* [11] lists the following numbers of programs in the United States and Canada in the areas indicated: computer science, 333; information science, 95; information systems, 72; and management information systems, 33.

On the basis of the number of accredited computer engineering programs (50 to 60) and the number of Ph.D.-granting computer engineering departments (34), it is estimated that there are about 40 master's programs in computer engineering.

The number of master's graduates in Ph.D.-granting computer science departments has averaged about 30 per department per year for the past five years [6], and the same holds for computer engineering departments. It seems likely that the average number of graduates would be smaller in non-Ph.D.-granting departments (because these departments are usually smaller than the Ph.D.-granting departments), and under this assumption an estimate of the annual production for master's degrees is about 9,000 in computer science and about 1,200 in computer engineering. *Science and Engineering In-*

dicators: 1989 [9] indicates that there were about 8,000 computer science master's graduates in 1986, and comparison and projection using the data in the Taulbee report [6] indicate that the estimate of 9,000 master's graduates in computer science is not unreasonable.

No data were found on the number of graduates in the other programs. However, under the assumption that the number of graduates produced annually per department should not be far from that for computer science and computer engineering, rough estimates are about 2,500 master's graduates in information science, 1,900 in information systems, and 900 in management information systems. Thus, there appear to be about 15,000 "computer specialists" who graduate with master's degrees annually.

One additional category of master's programs should be discussed: software engineering. Degree programs in software engineering are relatively new, but there are already 15 master's programs in existence, and at least 6 M.S. programs in computer science offer an option in software engineering [5]. Given that there were only three or four such programs five years ago, and one of those no longer exists, there might well be a significant number of these programs within five more years.

The growth of master's programs in software engineering has been stimulated by the Software Engineering Institute (SEI) at Carnegie Mellon University. The SEI has published curriculum recommendations for these programs [5] and has also produced a variety of materials to help faculty teach software engineering courses at the master's level.

Doctoral Programs

Doctoral programs in computing are offered in essentially the same major areas as are master's programs. Almost all of the degrees have the designation Ph.D. or an equivalent such as Sc.D., and they are research degrees. (That is, there are apparently no "professional" degree programs at the doctoral level.)

Excellent data on Ph.D. programs in computer science and computer engineering can be found in the Taulbee report [6]. There are 123 Ph.D. programs in computer science and 34 in computer engineering in the United States. These programs produced about 670 Ph.D. graduates in computer science and 170 in computer engineering in 1989-1990. The number of Ph.D. graduates in computer science tripled over the preceding six-year period, and the number of Ph.D. graduates in computer engineering experienced similar growth.

About 50 percent of the computer science doctoral graduates accept teaching and research positions in academia, and a little over 25 percent take industrial research and development positions, with about 15 percent in basic research [6] [9]. These percentages have been relatively constant over the past few years.

No corresponding data for doctoral programs in information science, information systems, and management information systems were found.

BACCALAUREATE PROGRAMS

Given the degree titles listed above for baccalaureate programs in computing and adding electrical engineering (E.E.; with computer emphasis) for convenience, one way to view general characteristics of typical programs in each category is shown in Figure B.1.

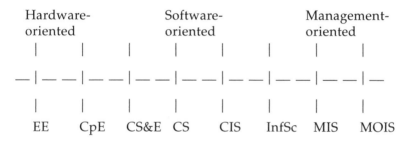

FIGURE B.1 It should be noted that the placement of information science (InfSc) is somewhat arbitrary. It is doubtful that information science programs are, in general, more management oriented than are computer information systems (CIS) programs, and so it might be more accurate to interchange CIS and InfSc in this scheme.

Unfortunately it is not possible to form such a characterization based on program titles because of the inconsistencies in their use. For example, there are programs called Management Information Systems (MIS) that span the range between computer information science and management of information systems (MOIS) in Figure B.1. Similarly, there are programs called Computer Science (CS) that span the range between computer engineering (CpE) and information science (or perhaps even management information systems). Thus it is difficult to discuss program characteristics on the basis of program titles.

On the basis of program objectives and characteristics, the baccalaureate programs of primary interest here can be grouped into four categories:

- Information systems
- Information science
- Computer science
- Computer engineering

It should be noted that each of these category names is intended to be relevant to and descriptive of the nature and characteristics of programs in that category, but not necessarily indicative of the titles of programs in the category. A degree program with a title that is similar to one of the category names usually falls into that category, but this is not always the case. The confusion between degree titles and category names could have been avoided by using different category names, but the names used here were chosen because they are fairly standard. Each category is discussed below, followed by a discussion of software engineering and computational science.

Information Systems

The category information systems includes most programs titled Information Systems and Computer Information Systems and many, if not most, of the programs titled Management Information Systems. Programs titled Management of Information Systems, and some titled Management Information Systems, produce, for the most part, graduates who are managers more than computer specialists. These latter programs are considered here as specialties in management rather than specialties in computing, and they are therefore not included in any of the categories of programs in computing here.

Peterson's [12] lists 106 programs in information systems and 53 programs in management information systems. However, a survey conducted on behalf of the Data Processing Management Association, which used the *Peterson's* list and other sources, generated a list of 1,002 programs in the United States and Canada to which the survey (about information systems curricula) was mailed [7]. The results of the survey listed 122 different program titles for "information systems" programs, but many of these, such as Accounting, Accounting Information Systems, Computer Science, Software Engineering, and Computer Engineering, clearly do not all represent programs that would normally be included in this category. It seems likely that there are at least 150 programs in this category, and there may be considerably more. No information was found regarding the number of graduates of these programs.

The Data Processing Management Association has recently published a report that contains recommendations for undergraduate programs in information systems [8]. The ACM also published curriculum recommendations for information systems programs in 1982 [10]. These documents specify that information systems curricula should include:

1. A reasonable core of basic computer concepts, including software development, computer hardware, algorithms and data structures, programming languages, operating systems, and data communications;

2. More advanced work in databases, information storage and retrieval, and software engineering;

3. Organizational concepts and systems theory; and

4. Work in basic business areas such as accounting, economics, finance, management, and marketing.

The coverage of computer concepts in an information systems program is usually more functionally oriented than is the case in a computer science/engineering program. That is, students in an information systems program are primarily interested in understanding the concepts of hardware and operating systems rather than in being able to build hardware or operating systems. This is not to say that there is no technical content to these programs or that they do not produce some graduates who can function quite well as, for example, systems programmers. However, the main focus of information systems programs is the development of software to solve managerial, financial, and other business problems.

There is quite a variation in the requirements and the level of quality in information systems programs. The number of courses in computing ranges from about 8 to 12 (semester courses), but these are sometimes more similar to service courses in computing than to courses taken by computer science majors. The good programs have strong computing components, however, and their rigorous requirements produce graduates who are well prepared to play leadership roles in software development and other activities involved in the application of computers to business problems.

Information Science

The computing components of information science programs are actually quite similar to the computing components of programs in information systems, although there is less variation in information science programs and their computing component is usually stronger than that of many information systems programs. Information science programs do not generally have the strong business component that is found in information systems programs, but the information science programs usually have a stronger emphasis on cognitive science. Additionally, strong programs in information science require solid decision science foundations, building on mathematics and statistics.

Peterson's [12] lists 143 undergraduate programs in information science. However, the programs included by *Peterson's* self-select the category in which to list their programs, and it seems likely that many of these are not information science programs as described here. No other data were found to indicate the number of programs or graduates. It appears that the title of most programs in this category is Information Science, and that the converse also holds.

Information science programs are often administered by the same academic unit as an institution's library science program. However, there is no longer any significant similarity between the two types of programs in most institutions.

Computer Science

Two significant sources help characterize computer science programs. A recent report published jointly by the ACM and the Computer Society of the Institute of Electrical and Electronics Engineers (IEEE-CS) provides curriculum recommendations for programs in computer science (and computer engineering as well) [13]. These recommendations apply to broad programs at liberal arts colleges as well as to more intensive programs in universities and colleges.

A second source can be found in the criteria for accreditation of programs in computer science [3]. These criteria provide specifications for programs that are intended to produce graduates who are prepared to enter the computing profession. Computer science accreditation is provided by the Computer Science Accreditation Commission of the Computing Sciences Accreditation Board. The accreditation criteria include requirements for at least 40 semester credits of computer science and at least 32 credits of mathematics and science.

The two curriculum specifications do not conflict. Both call for a broad base of fundamental work followed by appropriate advanced work. The ACM/IEEE-CS report specifies common requirements for all computing programs (including computer engineering) in terms of the subject material to be covered. This includes material from nine areas: (1) algorithms and data structures, (2) architecture, (3) artificial intelligence and robotics, (4) database and information retrieval, (5) human-computer communication, (6) numerical and symbolic computation, (7) operating systems, (8) programming languages, and (9) software methodology and engineering.

Additionally, substantial work in programming skills and in social, ethical, and professional issues is included. It should be noted that the coverage of the various areas is not even in the common requirements: some areas, such as human-computer communication and numerical and symbolic computation, are covered only in an introductory manner in the basic course work, while other areas, such as algorithms and data structures or architecture, receive more extensive coverage.

Good programs in computer science provide a solid foundation based on theoretical principles and concepts, and these principles and concepts are reinforced in extensive practical exercises and examples. Hands-on laboratory work, both structured and unstructured, is important. Graduates of a computer science program should be well grounded in the fundamental concepts and problem-solving skills needed to design and develop new applications, usually software, or to design and develop computer systems software and utility programs.

Peterson's [12] lists 1,058 programs in computer science. However, *Peterson's* not only allows institutions to designate the categories in which they have programs, but also allows multiple listings. Thus some programs in other areas, such as information systems, may also choose to be listed in computer science, and so it seems unlikely that there are 1,058 programs in computer science in the United States.

Based on the experience of the first six years of operation, the Computing Sciences Accreditation Board (CSAB) estimates that 200 to 400 programs may be appropriate for possible accreditation. (Currently there are 107 accredited programs at 106 institutions.) Additionally there are a good many programs at strong liberal arts colleges, but these colleges do not consider their programs to be professionally oriented so that accreditation is not appropriate. Many, if not most, of those programs would qualify as computer science programs as the category is intended here. There remain an undetermined number of very weak programs, whose computing components most often consist essentially of a few courses in programming, that may call themselves "computer science" but do not qualify under the characterization of that category here. We see, then, that there is a wide variation in the nature and quality of programs in computer science.

Science and Engineering Indicators: 1989 [9] shows 42,195 bachelor's graduates in computer science in 1986. Given the significant decline in graduates from most programs that has occurred since then, it seems reasonable to expect that the current annual number of graduates should be about 28,000 to 30,000. This would seem to indicate that about 1,000 programs is not unreasonable. However, it is not clear what definition was used for "computer science" here. Thus, the actual number of programs that fall into this category and the number of graduates of such programs are no clearer for computer science than for the other categories.

Computer Engineering

Programs in the computer engineering category differ from the others in one significant way: they require a basic engineering core of science, mathematics, and engineering science. Accreditation of engineering programs by the Engineering Accreditation Commission of the Accreditation Board for Engineering and Technology is generally accepted as important and expected. Currently there are 43 accredited programs titled Computer Engineering, and there are additional programs with alternative titles, such as Computer Science and Engineering, that are accredited under the criteria for computer engineering programs [1]. Thus probably about 60 programs fall into this category. Data on the number of graduates were not found.

The computing component for the computer engineering programs is essentially the same as for strong, professionally oriented programs in computer science. In general, the engineering programs tend to place more emphasis on computer hardware than do the computer science programs, and topics such as real-time systems and CAD/CAM are also more heavily emphasized in computer engineering.

Software Engineering

There apparently are no undergraduate programs in software engineering currently. However, some efforts have been made to move toward offering undergraduate degree programs in software engineering, and a few departments are considering doing so. The Software Engineering Institute has published curriculum recommendations for undergraduate software engineering programs [4].

Software engineering programs, as envisioned by the Software Engineering Institute recommendations, emphasize an engineering approach to developing software. Such programs would have substantial components in mathematics and science and would also include such subjects as project management and team management. Graduates of these programs would be familiar with basic concepts of computer science, but the programs would emphasize disciplined, engineering approaches to software development.

A great many, if not most, computer scientists in academia feel that software engineering is more appropriate as a track or concentration within a computer science (or computer engineering) program than as a separate degree program. However, there is increasing pressure from industrial and government representatives to address what they perceive to be an inadequacy in the capabilities of computer science graduates. A new DARPA program offers the possibility of substantial funding to initiate an undergraduate program in software engineering.

Computational Science

Computational science is an area that refers to the capabilities needed to work efficiently and effectively in the application of large-scale computing to problems in science. Subjects such as numerical computation, parallel computation, and significant work in science are important components. There are very few, if any, undergraduate programs in computational science currently.

The impetus for computational science programs came from physical and biological scientists who felt that computer science was not producing the capabilities needed to solve their computational problems. (This is similar to the impetus for software engineering programs.) Several efforts are under consideration to offer tracks within existing programs, or perhaps separate degree programs, in computational science, but most of this activity is confined to the graduate level.

COMPARISON OF BACCALAUREATE PROGRAMS

In summary, the following are characteristics of the baccalaureate program classifications given in the previous section:

1. Information Systems Programs

   - Have significant computing and business components.
   - Emphasize software development and information management in the computing component.
   - Are different from MOIS programs (more technical, less behavioral or functional).
   - Have curriculum recommendations [8] [10].
   - Have no program accreditation mechanism.
   - Produce graduates for information systems development.

2. Information Science Programs

   - Have significant computing, cognitive science, and decision science components.
   - Have substantial overlap of computing components with information systems programs.
   - Have no standard curriculum recommendations.
   - Have no program accreditation mechanism.
   - Produce graduates for information systems development, especially decision-oriented and highly interactive systems.

3. Computer Science Programs

   - Have a stronger and broader computing component than programs in the previous two categories.
   - Have stronger mathematics and science than the previous two categories.
   - Have standard curriculum recommendations [13].
   - Have an accreditation mechanism for professionally oriented programs [3].
   - Produce graduates for a variety of applications, depending on advanced work.

4. Computer Engineering Programs

   - Have significant computing and "engineering" components.
   - Have significant overlap with computer science in computing components.
   - Have standard curriculum recommendations [13].
   - Have an accreditation mechanism [1].
   - Produce graduates similar to those for professionally oriented computer science programs.

One way to view these four categories is that their intersection is in computer science, and that other categories represent specialties related to computer science. This view works better for information science and information systems than for computer engineering, because there is substantial overlap between computer engineering and the category computer science as defined here. Further, many, if not most, programs in the other categories include computer science courses in their curricular requirements. Thus computer science can be viewed as providing the primary subject-area basis for the other three categories.

SUMMARY FOR TWO-YEAR AND GRADUATE PROGRAMS

Two-Year Programs

The four categories that were used for baccalaureate programs are not good for the two-year programs. Appropriate categories for these programs were mentioned in "Overview of Programs" above.

One aspect of the two-year programs that is quite different from the baccalaureate programs is that many of the two-year programs are highly specialized or are oriented toward office functions. Examples are programs with titles such as CAD/CAM and Microprocessor Applications. Additionally, programs such as "Computer Service Technician" are not comparable to any four-year programs.

Two-year programs do include programs that would generally fall under the information systems and computer science categories. However, the two-year programs do not generally have the depth of course work in the major or the level of supporting science and mathematics course work that is found in baccalaureate programs. Two-year programs are usually intended to teach sufficient skills and current technology to allow graduates to obtain entry-level jobs.

Graduate Programs

Both master's and doctoral programs exist in information systems, information science, computer science, and computer engineering. There are also master's programs in software engineering and computational science, and doctoral programs in computational science. Many master's programs are professionally oriented (rather than research oriented) or have a professionally oriented track.

Some variations, such as programs specializing in telecommunications and decision support systems, are more prevalent at the graduate level than they are at the undergraduate level. These more specialized programs provide advanced work that is in general more focused than in most undergraduate programs, and they are usually professionally oriented.

CONCLUSIONS

Baccalaureate programs in computing generally fall into four categories: information systems, information science, computer science, and computer engineering. However, the title of a particular program does not necessarily indicate the category to which it belongs, because there is a great deal of variation in the titles of programs relative to their content.

Similar categories exist at the graduate level, but there are more specialized programs at the graduate level than at the undergraduate level. Examples are programs with software engineering, decision support systems, medical information systems, or telecommunications systems specializations. These may exist as tracks in more general programs, such as computer science or information science, or they may be separate degree programs.

The lack of any standardization for degree titles makes meaningful classification of graduates for reporting and analysis very difficult, if not essentially impossible. It should be noted that accreditation criteria for information systems and information science programs would help here. However, even the existence of an accreditation mechanism for these programs would not be effective without strong support from industry, and significant industrial support has not occurred for the existing computer science accreditation mechanism.

Another serious problem in trying to do a reasonable analysis of existing programs is the lack of data, especially meaningful data. Obtaining such data would be a formidable task, and it is doubtful that obtaining accurate data for the four categories identified for baccalaureate programs would be feasible. However, even having accurate data on such things as the number of programs and the number of graduates for various degree titles would be helpful in determining the nature of the products of U.S. degree programs in computing. It should also be noted that it would be feasible to develop good estimates of degree production for the four categories, but it would require a substantial effort to do so.

A final point is that what academic institutions are producing and what industry needs can be successfully identified only through cooperative efforts among academia, industry, and government. This may seem obvious, but it is stated to emphasize that, for example, industry cannot develop specifications for its needs without working with appropriate representatives on the academic side, because such a set of specifications would not be understood correctly by those in academia. Similarly, if academia attempts to design programs to meet the needs of industry without doing so in cooperation with industry, these efforts are bound to miss the mark. Industry participation is key here, because without clear interest and support from industry, neither academia nor government will be motivated to make the required effort to address the problem. Indeed, if there is no interest from industry, then it can be argued that there really is no problem.

REFERENCES

[1] Accreditation Board for Engineering and Technology (ABET), 1990. *Criteria for Accrediting Programs in Engineering in the United States.* Computing Science Accreditation Board, Inc., Stamford, Conn.

[2] Chronicle Data Publications, 1990. *Chronicle Two-Year College Databook.* Chronicle Press, Moravia, N.Y.

[3] Computing Sciences Accreditation Board (CSAB), 1990. *Criteria for Accrediting Programs in Computer Science in the United States.* Computing Science Accreditation Board, Inc., Stamford, Conn.

[4] Ford, G., 1990. *1990 SEI Report on Undergraduate Software Engineering Education.* Technical Report CMU/SEI-90-TR-3. Software Engineering Institute, Carnegie Mellon University, March.

[5] Ford, G., 1991. *1991 SEI Report on Graduate Software Engineering Education.* Technical Report CMU/SEI-91-TR-2. Software Engineering Institute, Carnegie Mellon University, April.

[6] Gries, D., and Marsh, D., 1991. "The 1989-1990 Taulbee Survey Report." *Computing Research News* 3(January):1.

[7] Longenecker, H.E., Jr., and Feinstein, D.L., 1991. "A Comprehensive Survey of USA and Canadian Undergraduate Programs in Information Systems." *Journal of Information Systems Education* 3 (Spring):1.

[8] Longenecker, H.E., Jr., and Feinstein, D.L. (eds.), 1991. *Information Systems.* Data Processing Management Association, Park Ridge, Ill.

[9] National Science Board, 1989. *Science and Engineering Indicators, 1989.* U.S. Government Printing Office, Washington, D.C.

[10] Nunamaker, J.F., Jr., Couger, J.D., and Davis, G.B. (eds.), 1982. "Information Systems Curriculum Recommendations for the 1980s: Undergraduate and Graduate Programs." *Communications of the ACM* 25 (November):11.

[11] *Peterson's Annual Guides to Graduate Study.* Vols. 1-6. Peterson's Guides, Inc., Princeton, N.J.

[12] *Peterson's Guide to Four-Year Colleges.* Peterson's Guides, Inc., Princeton, N.J.

[13] Tucker, A.B., et al., 1991. *Computing Curricula 1991.* ACM Press, New York.

C

The Demand For Human Resources and Skills in the 1990s

E.G. Nichols
IBM Corporation

How many computing professionals are needed and what specialties within the profession are most in demand? The outlook has been, and continues to be, that there will be a strong and increasing demand for computing professionals. Recent changes such as the recession, business consolidations, and peace may temper the demand, but overall the demand is still strong.

Many factors influence demand. The evolution of global markets, the rapid changes in technology, computer technology moving into the home and entertainment markets, and shifts in the type of work performed by computing professionals are all influencing demand.

In the 1990s success in this field will depend on highly skilled computing professionals properly equipped with productivity-enhancing electronic tools. It is time to consider a formal approach to skills planning as a means for companies, and perhaps countries, to project their needs for skills and to maintain their competitiveness.

NOTE: A paper prepared for a computer science and technology workshop sponsored by the Computer Science and Telecommunications Board and the Office of Scientific and Engineering Personnel of the National Research Council, and held at the National Academy of Sciences Beckman Center, Irvine, California, October 28-29, 1991.

THE ENVIRONMENT:
GENERAL BUSINESS TRENDS

Experts predict significant changes in the work force by the year 2000. Already there is evidence that these predictions are correct and that such changes may occur well before the year 2000.

Experts expect to see many international alliances. Already the political changes that will make this possible are occurring: the opening of Eastern European and the former USSR. The 1992 changes in Europe encourage alliances among European companies, and many predict even more open trading among nations in the Americas as well. The rate at which countries, previously closed to U.S. companies, are embracing free trade is staggering. In the wake of this rapid political change, international alliances offer solutions that one company cannot undertake alone. For example, companies in Japan and Germany are discussing alliances as a means to improve the communications systems for what was formerly known as East Germany.

As the world moves from the industrial age to the information age, information—and the tools for quickly analyzing and distributing that information—will be readily available at the workstation or desktop. Workers, with a large amount of information readily available, will broaden the scope of their work and acquire more skills; they will be multiskilled workers. The computer science and technology professions will provide the products and services to make this possible, and there will be a tremendous demand for those who can integrate powerful tools into the workplace.

The marketplace for the 1990s is a global, not a national, marketplace. Many of today's products have parts or components that are manufactured in one country, assembled or integrated in another country, and perhaps sold worldwide under a variety of logos or brand names. In the future, more and more products will be developed in this manner.

The work force must be highly educated; the work force must be competent in mathematics and communications (reading, writing, speaking, and listening) and must be motivated and capable of continuous learning. In addition, the work force needs to be computer literate. Although computers will continue to be easier to use, they will also be integrated into more and more products and services. And as computer technology improves, we will need more computer professionals to research, develop, and apply the technology to a wider and wider range of uses.

As the demand for products and services becomes a worldwide

demand and as new and improved products and services use computer technology increasingly, the demand for computer professionals will become a global demand: workers will migrate to jobs, and work will be moved to the people with the necessary skills. U.S. companies must be aware that they will be competing with other countries, not only other companies, as they seek to hire people with key skills in computer science. The number of foreign students in the graduate degree programs in U.S. universities is large and is increasing. Because of increasing global demand, these foreign students will have more employment options than they have had in the past, including returning to their home countries and emigrating to a third country to take advantage of the best opportunities.

Several developing countries are nurturing the development of computer technology and software. The combination of a strong educational system, government support, and a cheaper labor force is helping these efforts in India and China. This trend is significant in two ways: (1) U.S. firms may move their work (demand) to the available, skilled work force, and (2) a larger number of Chinese and Indian graduate students may find a larger number of options for challenging work in their home countries and return there rather than work in the United States.

ACADEMIA

Recent assessments of U.S. graduate degree programs in computer science have examined the faculty with respect to its strength, anticipated hiring, and other variables. The fields of computer science and computer engineering are new compared to other fields, and the faculty is younger. Thus, for the next 5 years the computer science and engineering departments will have fewer faculty openings resulting from retirement of current staff than other fields will experience. The college-age population has shrunk; fewer students are entering college, and of those entering fewer are choosing the computer fields. Recently there has been only a little growth in the number of faculty in computer fields, and this growth is expected to be 5 percent from 1991 through 1996. However, unfilled demand for computer science and engineering faculty still exists. This demand is expected to shrink somewhat and will be filled more selectively, but fewer new information systems doctorates will find positions in academia. Therefore, as long as other factors remain stable, no shortage in faculty is anticipated through the mid-1990s.

INFORMATION TECHNOLOGY

Past

In the early 1980s most of the computing complex was centralized logically and physically. Sites were connected, but usually in a hierarchy of smaller, remote sites individually attached electronically to a central computer room. In this environment the hardware, systems software, and application software were managed and controlled by a single information systems group. Although more than one vendor provided the various hardware and software products, the number of unique vendors that each installation dealt with was generally small. The attached networks were populated with "dumb" terminals whose applications resided on the host systems.

During this time the large backlog of applications requested but not yet delivered drove computer-literate professionals in science and engineering departments to acquire their own hardware and software solutions. If an information technology department could not deliver the needed applications quickly, it was often bypassed completely. The combination of a growing backlog of requested applications and the availability of minicomputers fueled the growth of this trend toward department systems. Next, personal computers became popular because of the relatively small investment needed to get started and because of the personal productivity tools they provided. But as individuals increased their productivity, they expanded their scope and sought additional functions—many of which (such as information kept on centralized databases) were available on the host system. New software and new applications had to be written for this new environment.

Many more vendors entered the field in the 1980s, especially vendors with customized offerings. The cost of entry was small for both hardware and software companies. For the hardware companies, with some exceptions, the parts were relatively easy to acquire. Many small software firms emerged with products aimed at particular business applications or environments.

Present

Now information technology groups have to cope with rapidly increasing complexity. First, they don't necessarily control the computing power of their companies because individuals and departments have bought a wide variety of personal computers and software that are distributed, not centralized. The communications links have grown rapidly with increased complexity, speed, number of connections, and number of different protocols. A large number of different vendors provide products and services in the 1990s environment, and the combinations are huge. This significantly increases the skills required to install, operate, and maintain these computing complexes.

The press has been full of news of mergers among tire companies, appliance companies, banks, and airlines. These mergers will affect their information technology organizations, reducing overall investments as consolidations occur and increasing complexity as diverse systems are integrated.

Future

By the mid-1990s, the leading-edge applications will run on very high speed integrated LANs and with powerful workstations and will have access to a large amount of data kept in data repositories. The interfaces will be standardized, but the underlying structure will continue to contain a variety of systems and communications links, and a proliferation of software and hardware products. Some of the applications and infrastructure from the 1980s and early 1990s will still exist and will need to be supported. There will be significant demand for new applications on the powerful workstations. Completely new approaches to application development (object-oriented programming and reuse) will involve tools to help information technology groups manage this very high degree of complexity.

Outlook for Information Technology Investment

The outlook for information technology spending through the mid-1990s is that actual dollars spent will increase, but the rate of spending will decline. In the past, spending on information technology has increased during recessions; however, in 1991 information technology has not been immune to the effects of recession. In comparing information technology spending in 1991 to the projected 1992 budgets, *Computer Economics* found that 22 percent of the companies surveyed expect a decline, 2 percent expect to stay the same, and the remaining 76 percent expect to grow. Also, the larger the company, the more likely it is to increase its information technology spending. Several information technology organizations report that the growth they are seeing is being driven by support for expanding international operations.

Spending on mainframes is declining. Of those with large glasshouse installations, today more are buying used mainframes or staying a generation behind to avoid the large investment needed to upgrade technology. The decline in spending on mainframes from 1990 to 1992 is expected to be 4 percent. The rest of the industry is expected to grow: small growth (4 percent) is expected for mid-range computers, moderate growth is expected for supercomputers (14 percent) and for personal computers (16 percent), and excellent growth is expected for workstations (66 percent).

Shifts in spending can be explained by shifts in the types of systems used for new applications. The development and implementation of new applications have shifted to the lower-cost workstations and personal computers, thus accounting for the slowing rates of spending. Further, a key measurement shows decline. Information technology spending as a percentage of a company's revenue is declining from 2.6 to 2.5 percent: the rate is declining for large and mid-sized companies and staying level for small companies.

Growth Areas

The several areas in which information technology will invest heavily over the next few years are the areas that cause the most problems today: systems integration and systems management. Spending related to systems integration is expected to grow by 22 percent per year, tripling between 1990 and 1995. The systems integration applications are being implemented differently as well. More and more large projects are subdivided into smaller steps. The smaller projects are delivered in a shorter time, and thus the cost is less. Real experience with the results of the smaller steps influences the next step of development, and thus the user's satisfaction with the total project is higher. Systems integration will definitely be a source of new jobs in information technology in the mid-1990s.

The other area of significant growth is systems management. This area is expected to grow by 17 percent between 1990 and 1995. The heterogeneous, distributed computing environment for the mid-1990s has many hidden difficulties. The workstations and personal computers distributed on LANs still need support. One estimate is that one person is needed to install, upgrade, move equipment, and resolve problems for each 25 workstations or personal computers on a LAN. Very often an undertrained individual in the end-user department is designated to do the work; in this case it is likely that the resource is never counted in the information technology totals. In addition, undertrained personnel make mistakes that often create large problems for information technology personnel to resolve. Many information technology organizations feel that distributed systems are a key part of their responsibility and maintain the control and support of these assets: these types of organizations will see growth in LAN support personnel as their distributed systems grow. Other groups that are frustrated by the complexity of the environment, or did not have the skilled personnel to assume control of the distributed systems that emerged, are looking to service companies to take over the management of this complex environment. When this is the case only the dollars will be visible in the information technology budget, but the human resource will reside in the new service company.

Salaries, the best indicator of whether computing professionals will be increased, are expected to increase only to keep pace with inflation from 1991 to 1992. However, as organizations outsource the operation of their central complex or even the management of their networks, additional resources will be added to the industry, but in the service companies.

Summary—Human Resources in Information Technology

With continuing growth but a slowing rate of growth in spending, and with a shift in the application environment from the mainframe computer to the workstation, what will be the impact on the prospects for computing professionals? The need for such professionals will also grow, but not as rapidly as in the past. New jobs will be added in the information technology organizations of new or small but growing companies. Large companies will add new jobs for systems integration and systems management. Also, new jobs will exist in service companies that offer to help existing information technology organizations to manage the dramatically more complex infrastructure.

Computing professionals will be expected to be more productive in the 1990s and will have more personal productivity tools such as workstations to help them. Operations will be increasingly automated, but the automation will be needed to keep abreast of the increasing complexity. New skills will be needed to handle the integration of heterogeneous systems and to manage large, complex communications systems. Application knowledge will be needed to tailor and customize applications to increasingly sophisticated users of computing. There will be a demand for increased numbers of computing professionals, but increased skills among the practitioners will be especially in demand.

RESEARCH AND DEVELOPMENT

Past

Computer hardware development has undergone considerable change in the last decade. As the hardware community developed new technologies such as large-scale integrated circuits, multiprocessors, microprocessors, and architectures, it did significant hiring. Hardware developers not only developed new technologies, but also developed the modeling, simulation, and design tools needed in these development efforts.

The resulting trends in price-performance ratios were dramatic. Between 1980 and 1985 the cost per million instructions per second (MIPS) fell from $250,000 to $25,000. The rate of improvement continued for the next 5 years, so that the cost per MIPS in 1990 was less than $2,500.

Present

The United States is seen as holding a leadership position in microprocessors, operating systems, user interfaces, databases, applications software, and magnetic information storage.

It is regarded as competitive in networks and communication, hardware integration, logic chips, submicro technology, and portable telecommunications.

The United States is behind in memory chips, optoelectronic components, optical information storage, electronic packaging and interconnections, displays, and hardcopy technology.

The shifts away from mainframe computers to workstations described above for information technology are true for research and development as well. The focus in the research and development communities has shifted from hardware to software and services. Many computer companies acknowledge this change and also indicate that they experience more shortages of people with software skills. One company reports that it takes twice as long to find a qualified software professional as it does to hire a hardware engineer. Another company notes that the rate of attrition for computer professionals in the first 5 years of employment has risen dramatically in recent years, showing that recent graduates with a small amount of industrial experience are in demand.

U.S. companies account for 57 percent of the worldwide software industry today, followed by Europe with 21 percent (France with 8 percent, Germany with 7 percent, and Britain with 6 percent), Japan with 13 percent, Canada with 3 percent, and other countries in Asia and Europe accounting for the remaining 6 percent.

Future

New Technologies

The future will see new technologies and the integration of existing technologies. Growth is expected for supercomputers, parallel architectures, multimedia, data storage and recall, natural language interfaces, pen-based operating systems, hand-held digital computers, digital video telecomputers, and speech and image recognition. Some of these new technologies will be integrated into cars, home appliances, and home entertainment systems.

Solutions to Current Problems

Much development work will be focused on reducing complexity, especially in developing already integrated solutions and in simplifying the systems management of large heterogeneous systems and networks.

Applications

In the computer industry now and through the mid-1990s, demand will focus on effectively using the computing power available on powerful workstations. In demand will be integrated solutions that specifically address unique needs: customized integration of a variety of products and applications tailored to specific industry needs. Because there is significant computing power available, there will be significant pressure to develop these customized solutions much more quickly than in the past.

Applications developers will be in demand in the computer industry. Computing professionals will need to understand the needs of end users by industry, by common types of work that cut across industries, and individually.

Client-server applications and programmers skilled in developing these applications are in short supply, and products are needed to distribute and update software on multiple workstations. In addition, the continuing large backlog of needed applications will fuel the demand for productivity improvements in systems and application development.

End-User Productivity

Any technology, hardware or software, that improves the productivity of end users or relates to the human interface will be important. Examples of such technologies include animation, full-motion video, graphics, image technology, pen technology and handwriting recognition, and audio technology and speech recognition.

Also, technology related to the productivity of end users will be important, for example, artificial intelligence, expert systems, natural language, and standardized interfaces.

Software Development Productivity

There is now widespread understanding that high quality leads to short cycle time and higher productivity. To address quality, computing professionals need (1) an understanding of the development process and its effect on quality, (2) integrated tools to make the development process efficient, (3) knowledge of the design practices that lead to high quality, and (4) the ability to engineer and institutionalize quality into software development. Very little is taught in the universities about the development process needed to engineer quality into large, complex software projects. Most of this knowledge is acquired on the job or through training programs in industry. Very often tools are separate, not integrated. By the mid-1990s there will be more life-cycle tools, architectures, and platforms that will enhance software developer productivity. Other new technologies are expected to improve productivity as well, including object-oriented programming and program reuse.

An important ingredient for achieving higher quality is design expertise. This skill is generally taught in software engineering curriculums found in advanced-degree programs. Currently many colleges and universities teach software engineering courses, but only 15 universities offer a master's degree in software engineering; none offers a B.S. Finding qualified software engineers is becoming more difficult.

DEMAND IN THE UNITED STATES

Will there be a shortage of engineers or scientists in the computing professions in the 1990s? During the 1980s the computer industry in the United States increased its employment by 68 percent, from 728,000 to 1.2 million. Although most companies were able to hire people with the skills they needed, they sometimes had problems finding particular skills. The Labor Department estimates that the demand for software professionals will double between 1991 and the year 2000. Looking beneath these numbers reveals significant shifts. In the research and development segment the shift emphasizes professionals skilled in software rather than hardware. The older established companies are growing at a slower rate than some of the new or emerging companies. The newer companies are more focused on software and services.

The hiring practices of large and small companies vary. Some small companies report that they cannot afford the expense of college recruiting. The smaller companies either target their hiring to a small number of universities or hire experienced personnel.

The larger companies generally recruit on many campuses. They find fewer graduates interested in or trained on the more stable technologies that the established companies need to maintain. When recruiting for open systems skills such as UNIX-based development, they find qualified candidates.

A survey conducted by Siegel and co-workers, of the Software Engineering Institute and School of Urban and Public Affairs, Carnegie Mellon University, found that defense industry executives and government officials felt skills shortages had been important factors contributing to the failure of military system development contracts to meet schedule or costs. Skills shortages were second only to inadequate requirements, specifications, and changes in requirements. Cited were shortages of systems engineers, software managers, qualified project managers, software engineers, and (of lesser impact) application domain experts. The SEI report further describes current shortages in application domain and software engineering expertise and the growing demand for resources to maintain the current systems.

GLOBAL COMPETITION AND DEVELOPMENT PRODUCTIVITY

Currently Japan has a shortage of 500,000 programmers and systems engineers that is expected to grow to 1 million by the year 2000. Japanese companies are establishing operations in other countries (the People's Republic of China, Malaysia, Singapore, India, and the Philippines) to fill their demand. There are 200,000 highly skilled programmers in China, with local demand for only 10,000. Some of India's leading software professionals have given up jobs elsewhere and returned to India, where 360 firms say they do some software development and another 250 firms define themselves as data processors. U.S. companies are also outsourcing software development in India, Singapore, and Korea.

In addition, the Japanese government is funding research to improve programmer productivity. To combat shortages of skilled programmers in Europe, 14 companies and institutes from five countries are working together to automate computer programming on a project named the Eureka Software Factory.

SUMMARY

The computer science and technology field will continue to grow for the next 5 years. For information technology, jobs will be added in systems integration and systems management; in research and development, new opportunities will be found in software and services, in the development of client-server applications, and in development efforts to simplify the information technology environment, to standardize and improve the human interface, and to improve development productivity.

BIBLIOGRAPHY

"Can the U.S. Stay Ahead in Software?" *Business Week,* March 11, 1991.

"Client Server Users See Tough Times Ahead." *Network World,* January 28, 1991.

"Client/Server Software Lags." *Computer Systems News,* February 11, 1991.

Corbi, Thomas A. "Findings: Software Process and Academia." *IBM Research,* Hawthorne, N.Y., April 1991.

Eaton, Catherine. "Redressing the Balance." *Systems International (UK),* October 1988.

Eerkes, Gary L. "Computer Science Master's Programs." *Communications of the ACM,* Vol. 34, No. 1, Jan. 1991.

"Eureka May Be Europe's Ticket to Sovereignty." *Business Week,* March 11, 1991.

"Feeling the Economic Pinch—IS Purchasing Plans Start to Account for Flat Spending." *Information Week,* October 7, 1991.

Finn, Michael G. "Personnel Shortage in Your Future?" *Research Technology Management,* Jan.-Feb. 1991, pp. 24-27.

Goldstein, Gina. "Joseph F. Coates: Engineering in the Year 2000." *Mechanical Engineering,* October 1990.

"Is Outsourcing the Answer?" *Information Week,* July 29, 1991.

"Japan Stakes Future on Research Co-ops." *Information Week,* July 3, 1989.

Jaruenpaa, Sirkka L., Blake Ives, and Gordon B. Davis. "Supply/Demand of I/S Doctorates in the 1990's." *Communications of the ACM,* Vol. 34, No. 1, Jan. 1991.

Kandebo, Stanley W. "Engineer Shortfall Still Seen, Despite Industry Doldrums." *Aviation Week and Space Technology,* March 4, 1991.

Lee, Dinah. "India's Becoming the New Asian Magnet for U.S. Business." *Business Week,* May 1, 1989.

Lucky, Robert W. "Engineering Education and Industrial Research and Development—the Promise and the Reality." *IEEE Communications Magazine,* December 1990, pp. 16-22.

Nolan, Richard L. "The Knowledge Work Mandate." *Stage by Stage,* Vol. 10, No. 2, March-April 1991.

Oshima, Keichi, and Keichi Yamada. "Continuing Engineering Education in Japan." *European Journal of Engineering Education,* Vol. 10, No. 3 & 4, 1985.

Rappaport, Andrew S., and Smuel Halevi. "The Computerless Computer Company." *Harvard Business Review,* July-August 1991.

Reich, Robert B. "Who Is Them?" *Harvard Business Review,* March-April 1991.

Siegel, J.A.L. *National Software Capacity Study.* Software Engineering Institute and School of Urban and Public Affairs, Carnegie Mellon University, February 1991.

Siegel, J.A.L., S. Stewman, S. Konda, P.D. Larleey, and W.G. Wagner. *National Software Capacity: Near-Team Study.* Software Engineering Institute and School of Urban and Public Affairs, Carnegie Mellon University, May 1990.

Tapia, Robert. "In Search of the Ideal Operator." *Computing Canada.* June 23, 1988.

Valigra, Lori. "Japan's Programmer Crunch." August 26, 1991.

Workforce 2000, Competing in a Seller's Market: Is Corporate America Prepared? Hudson Institute, Towers Perrin, August 1990.

D

Workshop Program

Monday, October 28

CONTINENTAL BREAKFAST (Refectory) AND REGISTRATION (Lecture Room)	8:00 a.m.

1. Welcome and Round-robin Introductions
   —Leslie L. Vadasz   9:00 a.m.

2. Three Overview Presentations   9:30 a.m.
- What the data and statistics show about computer specialists—Betty M. Vetter
- Supply of computer specialists: post-secondary degree programs—A. Joe Turner

BREAK   10:30 a.m.

- Demand for computer specialists: an industry perspective—Betty Nichols   11:00 a.m.

LUNCH (Refectory)   12:00 p.m.

3. Marketplace Demand and Occupational Mobility   1:00 p.m.

Panel chair: Robert Weatherall, Massachusetts
    Institute of Technology
Steering committee liaison: Shelby Stewman

This panel is concerned with employers' needs, hiring trends, and personnel flows, including career paths and adjustments to changing opportunities. What do computer specialists do and where do they go?

(Explore issues for research, applications, and deployment of talent pools.)

Panelists:
Tora Bikson, The RAND Corporation
Chris Caren, Lockheed Corporation
Bill Eaton, Amoco Canada
Gordon Eubanks, Symantec Corporation
Peter Freeman, Georgia Institute of Technology
Joe Kubat, New York Stock Exchange
Paul Maritz, Microsoft Corporation
Paula Stephan, Georgia State University
Paul Stevens, Hughes Aircraft Company

BREAK   3:00 p.m.

4. Data and Taxonomy   3:30 p.m.

Panel chair: Alan Fechter, National Research Council
Steering committee liaison: Paul Young

This panel is concerned with the ability to measure, monitor, and understand conditions and trends in computer specialist labor markets. How well do we know what we know, and how can we do better?

(Explore issues for research, applications, and deployment of talent pools.)

Panelists:
David Gries, Cornell University
Betty Nichols, IBM Corporation

Ian Rose, IBR Consulting Services Ltd.
Jane Siegel, Software Engineering Institute,
    Carnegie Mellon University
A. Joe Turner, Clemson University
Betty M. Vetter, Commission on Professionals
    in Science and Technology
Barbara Wamsley, National Academy of
    Public Administration
Brenda Wallace, Bureau of Labor Statistics

5. Preliminary Conclusions, Cross-cutting Issues
    —Les Vadasz and steering committee   5:00 p.m.

RECEPTION AND DINNER (Atrium)   5:30 p.m.

Tuesday, October 29 **(Lecture Room)**

CONTINENTAL BREAKFAST (Refectory)   8:00 a.m.

6. Pipeline for Talent and Equality of Opportunity   8:30 a.m.

Panel chair: Paul Young
Steering committee liaisons: Nancy Leveson
    and Jim Tennison

This panel is concerned with the supply of entry-level
personnel, including quantity, quality, and composition
(demographics).

(Explore issues for research, applications, and deployment
of talent pools.)

Panelists:
Peter Freeman, Georgia Institute of Technology
Bob Kraut, Bell Communications Research
Bill Lupton, Morgan State University
Lucy Suchman, Xerox Corporation, Palo Alto
    Research Center
Richard Tapia, Rice University
Brenda Wallace, Bureau of Labor Statistics

BREAK   10:00 a.m.

7. Training: Adequacy and Implications for Change   10:30 a.m.

Panel chair: Linda Pierce, Shell Oil Company
Steering committee liaisons: Maxine Trentham and
  Eileen Collins

This panel is concerned with the potential for education and
training to improve the fit of supply to demand, for all types
of computer specialists.

(Explore issues for research, applications, and deployment
of talent pools.)

Panelists:
Wade Ellis, West Valley College
Bill Gear, NEC Research Institute Inc.
Don McLean, Insurance Corporation of British Columbia
John McSorley, Apple Computer Inc.
Ian Rose, IBR Consulting Services Ltd.
Melissa Smartt, Sandia National Laboratories
Jim Williams, University of Pittsburgh
Marv Zelkowitz, University of Maryland

LUNCH (Refectory)   12:00 p.m.

8. Conclusions, Synthesis, and Directions:
What Have We Learned?   1:00 p.m.
    Leslie L. Vadasz, panel chairs, and
    steering committee

What can we do to better understand these labor markets?
What are next steps for broadening supply and enhancing
    the fit between supply and demand?

ADJOURN   3:00 p.m.